'RESERVATION IN SC, ST, OBC- SERVICE MATTER- SUPREME COURT'S LATEST LEADING CASE LAWS

CASE NOTES- FACTS- FINDINGS OF APEX COURT JUDGES & CITATIONS

JAYPRAKASH BANSILAL SOMANI

Dedicated

To

All the Past & Present Judges of the Supreme Court of India.

Salute to their wisdom.

Salute to their interpretation of Law.

Salute to their elaborative judgement writing.

ᐯᐯᐯ

Contents

Preface   *vii*

Acknowledgements   *ix*

1. Pankaj Kumar Vs. State Of Jharkhand And Ors., 2021   1

2. Chebrolu Leela Prasad Rao And Ors. Vs. State Of A.p. And Ors., 2020   4

3. Saurav Yadav And Ors. Vs. State Of Uttar Pradesh And Ors., 2020   11

4. Tamil Nadu Medical Officers Association And Ors. Vs. Union Of India (uoi) And Ors., 2020   14

5. Director Transport Department, Union Territory Administration Of Dadra And Nagar Haveli Silvassa And Ors. Vs. Abhinav Dipakbhai Patel, 2019   18

6. Sanjai Kumar And Ors. Vs. Prabhat Kumar And Ors., 2019   21

7. Anupal Singh And Ors. Vs. State Of U.p. And Ors., 2019   25

8. B.k. Pavitra And Ors. Vs. The Union Of India (uoi) And Ors., 2019   28

9. Govt. Of Nct Delhi And Ors. Vs. Pradeep Kumar And Ors., 2019   33

10. Niravkumar Dilipbhai Makwana Vs. Gujarat Public Service Commission And Ors., 2019   36

11. Tamil Nadu Medical Officers' Association And Ors. Vs. Union Of India (uoi) And Ors., 2018   39

12. B.k. Pavitra And Ors. Vs. Union Of India (uoi) And Ors., 2017   42

13. State Of U.p. And Ors. Vs. Dinesh Singh Chauhan, 2016   49

14. S. Panneer Selvam And Ors. Vs. Government Of Tamil Nadu And Ors., 2015   57

15. Chairman And Managing Director Central Bank Of India Vs. Central Bank Of India Sc/st Employees Welfare Association, 2015   61

16. U.p. Power Corporation Ltd. And Ors. Vs. Rajesh Kumar And Ors., 2012   64

17. Anil Chandra And Ors. Vs. Radha Krishna Gaur And Ors., 2009   69

18. Shiv Prasad Vs. Government Of India And Ors., 2008   72

Contents

19. Nair Service Society Vs. Dist. Officer, Kerala Public Service   75
    Commission And Ors., 2003

20. State Of Bihar And Ors. Vs. Bal Mukund Sah And Ors., 2000   79

Videos & Tv Shows On Law & Exim   83

List Of Adv. Jayprakash Somani's Books   89

Preface

Dear Learned Advocates of the Trial Courts, Tribunals, Appellate Tribunals, High Courts, Supreme Court, HR Professionals, Corporates, Govt Recruitment Officers & Employees,

I am very delighted to provide you a book on 'Reservation in SC, ST, OBC- Service Matter - Supreme Court of India's Latest Leading Case Laws'.

In this book you will get...

1. Name of the Case i. e. Cause title

2. Relevant Sections discussed in the case

3. Hon'ble Judges/Coram of the case

4. Number of PDF Pages in Original Judgement of the case

5. All available Citations of the case

6. Case Note with appeal allowed/ dismissed or disposed off

7. Facts of the case

8. Hon'ble Apex Court's findings, while dismissing/allowing or disposing the appeal

9. Ratio Decidendi if any.

My special thanks to Manupatra, because of their web portal I can compile this book in well manner. I am also thankful to Notion Press to support me to publish & market this book throughout the Country. Thanks to my Juniors, Advocate Colleagues & Insolvency Professional Colleagues to support me in this venture.

Miss Devpriya Shah has helped me a lot to compile this book.

I hope this book will add some value addition in the wealth of your legal knowledge. Your positive feedbacks will boost me to compile/ write further books & negative feedbacks will improve my skills. Kindly send your valuable feedbacks by email.

Thanks with Regards,

Jayprakash B. Somani

Advocate, Supreme Court of India

Email: jaysomani64@gmail.com

Web Site: www.jayprakashsomani.com

Call: 8384051134, 9322188701, 8459194576

ᘓᘓᘓ

Acknowledgements

Acknowledgement
Printed & Published by
Notion Press
No. 8, 3rd Cross Street,
CIT Colony, Mylapore,
Chennai, Tamil Nadu- 600004
Managed by
Jayprakash Somani Advocates & Solicitors
Law Firm for Supreme Court of India
Delhi Office
257 C, Pocket 1, Mayur Vihar Phase 1, Delhi 110091.
Call 8384051134, 9322188701, 8459194576, 01141051516
Supreme Court Chamber
312, 3rd Floor, M. C. Setalvad Block, In front of 'D' Gate, Bhagwan Das
Road, Supreme Court of India, New Delhi 110001
Contact: 8459194576, 9811011747
www.jayprakashsomani.com

ᐅᐅᐅ

Books are available online in India
1. Notion Press:https://notionpress.com/author/jayprakash_somani
2. Amazon:https://www.amazon.in/s?k=jayprakash+somani
3. Flipkart:https://www.flipkart.com/search?q=Jayprakash%20Somani
Books are available online at International Market
4. Amazon International: https://www.amazon.com/
s?k=jayprakash+somani
5. Amazon United Kingdom: https://www.amazon.co.uk/
s?k=jayprakash+somani
6. E-Books/Kindle edition at National & International Level:
https://www.amazon.in/s?k=jaypraksh+somani

ONE

PANKAJ KUMAR VS. STATE OF JHARKHAND AND ORS., 2021

Hon'ble Judges/Coram:

U.U. Lalit and Ajay Rastogi, JJ.

Equivalent Citation: 2021(5)BLJ198, 2021(3)PLJR444, 2021(3)SCT645(SC), 2021(3)SLJ310(SC), MANU/SC/0541/2021

Relevant sections: Constitution (Scheduled Castes)/(Scheduled Tribes) Order, 1950; Section 23, 24 and 73 of Bihar Reorganisation Act, 2000

Number of pages in original Judgment: 16

Case Note:

Constitution - Rights and privileges - Constitution (Scheduled Castes)/(Scheduled Tribes) Order, 1950 - Bihar Reorganisation Act, 2000(Act, 2000) - Resident of Bihar after bifurcation of State into Jharkhand - Appellant excluded from selection in Combined Civil Services Examination - Reserved category - Appellant denied benefit in Jharkhand otherwise available in Unified Bihar - Validity thereof - Whether Appellant incorrectly denied extension of benefits of being member of Scheduled Caste/Scheduled Tribe?

Brief Facts:

In the instant appeal (Civil Appeal @ SLP (Civil) No. 13473 of 2020), the Appellant's father originally belonged to District Patna in the State of Bihar. However, as alleged, the Appellant was born on 27th November, 1974 in Hazaribagh where his father was residing which earlier was part of the unified State of Bihar but after the Act, 2000came into force, District Hazaribagh became part of the successor State of Jharkhand.He belongs to Scheduled Caste category. He was appointed on the post of Assistant Teacher and posted in a school in Ranchi, Jharkhand against the post reserved for SC category. Pursuant to the cadre revision on bifurcation of the States, he opted the State of Jharkhand. While serving as a teacher, he successfully appeared as a member of SC category in the third Combined Civil Services examination, 2008. However his appointment order was withheld and persons lower in order of merit were appointed. He did not receive any response to query for non-inclusion. In the challenge made, he was held to be ineligible for appointment.

Held, while allowing the Appeals:

i. Employees who are members of the SC/ST/OBC whose caste/tribe has been notified by an amendment to the Constitution (Scheduled Castes)/(Scheduled Tribes) Order 1950 under Vth and VIth Schedule to Sections 23 and 24 of the Act 2000 or by the separate notification for members of other backward class category, benefit of reservation including privileges and benefits flowing thereof, shall remain protected by virtue of Section 73 of the Act 2000 for all practical purposes which can be claimed (including by their wards) for participation in public employment.

ii. Person is entitled to claim benefit of reservation in either of the successor State of Bihar or State of Jharkhand, but will not be entitled to claim benefit of reservation simultaneously in both the successor States and those who are members of the reserved category and are resident of the successor State of Bihar, while participating in open selection in State of Jharkhand shall be treated to be migrants and it will be open to participate in general category without claiming the benefit of reservation and vice-versa.

iii. Appellant in Civil Appeal @ SLP (Civil) No. 13473 of 2020entitled to claim the benefit of reservation including the privileges and benefits admissible to the members of Scheduled Caste category in the State of Jharkhand for all practical purposes including participation in open competition seeking public employment. Judgment of the High Court impugned dated 24th February, 2020 unsustainable and set aside.

🍂🍂🍂

TWO

CHEBROLU LEELA PRASAD RAO AND ORS. VS. STATE OF A.P. AND ORS., 2020

Hon'ble Judges/Coram:

Arun Mishra, Indira Banerjee, Vineet Saran, M.R. Shah and Aniruddha Bose, JJ.

Equivalent Citation: 2020(3)BLJ587, 2020(2)ESC527(SC), 2020(2)J.L.J.R.206, 2020(2)PLJR387, 2020(6)SLR558(SC), MANU/SC/0384/2020

Relevant sections: Article 14 of the Constitution of India; Sections 78 and 79 of the A.P. Education Act, 1982; Sections 169, 195, and 268 of the A.P. Panchayati Raj Act, 1994

Number of pages in original Judgment: 72

Case Note:

Constitution - Reservation - Denial of - Government order issued directing posts of teachers in educational institutions in scheduled tribe areas shall be reserved for Scheduled Tribes only - Another G.O. was issued to allow appointment of non-tribals to hold posts of teachers in scheduled areas till such time qualified local tribals were not made available - After that, non-tribals who were appointed as teachers in scheduled areas - Writ Petition was filed in High Court against termination of their services and same was allowed - In writ appeal, order of Single Bench was set aside by

Division Bench - Non-tribal appointees preferred Civil Appeal before this Court, which was allowed - After this Court rendered decision, Government issued fresh notification providing for hundred percent reservation in respect of appointment to posts of teachers in scheduled areas - Tribunal set aside GOMs - Aggrieved thereby, writ petitions were filed in High Court, which upheld validity of G.O - Hence, present appeal - Whether notification providing for hundred percent reservation in respect of appointment to posts of teachers in scheduled areas was unconstitutional.

Brief Facts:

By G.O. issued by the Governor in exercise of power under para 5(1) of Schedule V to the Constitution of India, directing the posts of teachers in educational institutions in the scheduled tribe areas shall be reserved for Scheduled Tribes only notwithstanding anything contained in any other order or Rule or law in force. The Andhra Pradesh Administrative Tribunal quashed the notification. The order was questioned in this Court which was dismissed as withdrawn. Another G.O. was issued to amend GOMs. to allow the appointment of non-tribals to hold the posts of teachers in the scheduled areas till such time the qualified local tribals were not made available. After that, non-tribals who were appointed as teachers in the scheduled areas. The Writ Petition was filed in the High Court against termination of their services. The same was allowed and GOMs. the advertisements were held to be violative of Article 14 of the Constitution of India. In writ appeal, the order of the Single Bench was set aside by the Division Bench. The non-tribal appointees preferred Civil Appeal before this Court, which was allowed. After this Court rendered the decision, the Government issued a fresh notification vide GOMs. effectively providing for hundred percent reservation in respect of appointment to the posts of teachers in the scheduled areas. The tribunal set aside the GOMs. Aggrieved thereby, writ petitions were filed in the High Court, which upheld the validity of G.O. The majority view opined that historically scheduled areas were treated specially, and affirmative action taken was in the constitutional spirit. The notification was a step for increasing literacy in the scheduled areas and also aimed at providing the availability of teachers in every school in the scheduled areas. The hundred percent reservation can be sustained on the ground that it was based on intelligible differentia, and the classification had nexus with the object sought to be achieved. The G.O. became necessary considering the phenomenal absenteeism of the teachers in the schools situated in the scheduled areas and was a step in aid to promote educational developments of tribals. In extraordinary situations, reservation could exceed fifty percent. The Governor possessed the power to issue the impugned notification under Schedule V, para 5(1) of the Constitution. The same overrides all other provisions of the Constitution, including Part III of the Constitution of India.

Held, while allowing the appeals:

i. The exceptions and modifications were created by the law, which is already applicable in the area. It is not the formulation of a new law which is contemplated under Para 5(1) of Schedule V. No new law could be formulated while exercising power under Para 5(1) of Schedule V. The power of modification could not extend to re-writing the entire statute. The power could not be used to supplant the law, which was applicable. The law had to be applied only with exceptions or modifications. It could not totally supersede the existing law, which was wholly opposed to the idea of applicable law as in that case it would tantamount to the new law and not the modification or exception or creation of exceptions or modifications to the applicable law. The object and substance of law applicable cannot be changed within the purview of Para 5(1), though the applicability of applicable law could be excluded. In case the Governor decides the law to remain applicable, he had the power only to create exceptions and to modify the same, not to create a new one juxtaposed to the same applicable law.

ii. The A.P. Regulation of Reservation and Appointment to Public Services Act, 1997, deals with reservation in the State in the field of public services. G.O. did not amend the said Act. The provisions of the other Acts mentioned in the notification did not deal with the extent of reservation. Sections 78 and 79 of the A.P. Education Act, 1982 and Sections 169, 195, and 268 of the A.P. Panchayati Raj Act, 1994, were not related to reservation. The Rules were framed under the proviso to Article 309. They were not framed under the main provision by the legislature. The Governor in the exercise of power under Para 5(1) of Schedule V could have amended the Public Services Act, 1997, or direct it not to apply to Scheduled Areas. The creation of hundred per cent reservation had the effect of making a new law under Para 5(1) without reference to the Act of State or Central legislation. Independently of that power could not be exercised within the purview of Para 5(1) of Schedule V to the Constitution of India. Even otherwise, even if the Act of 1997 would have been modified by the Governor, hundred percent reservation could not have been provided.

iii. The Governor's power to make new law is not available in view of the clear language of Para 5(1), Fifth Schedule does not recognise or confer such power, but only power was not to apply the law or to apply it with exceptions or modifications. Thus, notification was ultra vires to Para 5(1) of Schedule V of the Constitution.

iv. The Rules framed under the proviso to Article 309 of the Constitution could not be said to be the Act of Parliament or State legislature. Though the Rules had the statutory force, they cannot be said to have been framed under any Act of Parliament or State legislature. The Rules remain in force till such time the legislature exercises power. The power of the Governor under Para 5(1) of Schedule V of the Constitution is restricted to modifying or not to apply, Acts of the Parliament or legislature of the State. Thus, the Rules could not have been amended in the exercise of the powers conferred under Para 5(1) of Schedule V. The Rules made under proviso to Article 309 of the Constitution cannot be said to be an enactment by the State legislature. Thus, it was not open to the Governor to issue the impugned G.O.

v. The power was conferred on the Governor to deal with the scheduled areas. It was not meant to prevail over the Constitution. The power of the Governor was pari passu with the legislative power of Parliament and the State. The legislative power could be exercised by the Parliament or the State subject to the provisions of Part III of the Constitution. The power of the Governor did not supersede the fundamental rights under Part III of the Constitution. It had to be exercised subject to Part III and other provisions of the Constitution. When Para 5 of the Fifth Schedule confers power on the Governor, it was not meant to be conferral of arbitrary power. The Constitution could never aim to confer any arbitrary power on the constitutional authorities. They were to be exercised in a rational manner keeping in view the objectives of the Constitution. The powers were not in derogation but the furtherance of the constitutional aims and objectives.

vi. Considering the geographical disparity in public employment, Article 371D was inserted in the Constitution, providing candidates from certain districts/zones to form the local cadre for different posts for different parts of the States. The Presidential Order was issued providing district/ zone for local cadre, on the other hand, the order issued by the Governor has reserved all the posts of teachers in the Scheduled Areas for Schedule Tribe candidates. The aspiring candidates of the district/zone in the Scheduled Area could not apply for the post of teachers in the district as hundred per cent reservation was made vide G.O. by the Governor. It was also not disputed that aspiring candidates cannot apply outside the district/zone because of the restrictions under Article 371D of the Constitution. As there was hundred per cent reservation provided for the Scheduled Tribes in the Scheduled Areas, other candidates of Scheduled Castes, General and Other Backward Classes category cannot apply at all in other districts. They were being denied the opportunity of getting the employment as against the posts in question. Thus, the order issued by the Governor was clearly in conflict with the Presidential Order issued under Article 371D. The candidates of local areas or other candidates except for Scheduled Tribes had been deprived of the opportunity of seeking public employment because of the order issued by the Governor, and they could not apply outside the local area in view of the Presidential notification. The Presidential notification intends that they had to apply within the district, and the Governor's notification takes away that right. Thus, there was a clear repugnancy between the notification issued by the President and that subsequent order issued by the Governor in the exercise of powers under Para 5, Fifth Schedule of the Constitution. It was not possible to harmonise both the notifications. Apart from that, there was total deprivation. It was not factually correct that Presidential Order did not deal with Scheduled Areas. The Presidential Order applied to the entire State and carved out a special provision that applies with a non-obstante clause.

vii. The Governor was competent to issue an order which is not in conflict with the Presidential Order. The Governor issued the order when the Presidential Order was already in force in the entire State. The Governor could not have issued the order in derogation to the Presidential Order. The hundred per cent reservation could not have been provided as that violates the Presidential Order.

viii. By providing hundred percent reservation to the scheduled tribes has deprived the scheduled castes and other backward classes also of their due representation. The concept of reservation was not proportionate but adequate, as held in Indra Sawhney. The action was thus unreasonable and arbitrary and violative of provisions of Articles 14, 15 and 16 of the Constitution of India. It also impinges upon the right of open category and scheduled tribes who have settled in the area. The total percentage of reservation provided for Scheduled Tribes in the State was six percent. By providing hundred percent reservation in the scheduled areas, the rights of the tribals, who are not residents of the scheduled areas, shall also be adversely affected. As per Presidential order under Article 371-D, they could not stake their claim in other areas. The posts in other areas are to be reduced by making a hundred reservation in a particular area.

ix. A reservation that was permissible by protective mode, by making it hundred percent would become discriminatory and impermissible. The opportunity of public employment could not be denied unjustly to the incumbents, and it was not the prerogative of few. The citizens had equal rights, and the total exclusion of others by creating an opportunity for one class was not contemplated by the founding fathers of the Constitution of India. Equality of opportunity and pursuit of choice under Article 51-A could not be deprived of unjustly and arbitrarily. As per the Presidential Order, the citizens of the locality and outsiders were entitled to fifteen percent of employment in the district cadre in terms of Clause 10 of Article 370(1) (d) of the Constitution. Thus, the G.O. did not classify but deals with reservations. It was contrary to the report sent to the President by the Governor, which indicated even the posts which were reserved for scheduled tribes teachers, they were not available as such Tribes Advisory Council decided to fill them from other non-local tribals.

x. It was not in dispute that the district is a local area and a unit for the appointment of teachers and reservation is provided at the district level and as per the Presidential Order under Article 371D of the Constitution, incumbent of one district cannot stake claim outside the district for an appointment. The reservations for scheduled tribes are covered within the ken of Article 16(4). Thus, no further preference or classification could have been made under Article 16(1) of the Constitution of India in favour of scheduled tribes as Article 16(4) was exhaustive of the special provisions that can be made in favour of scheduled castes, scheduled tribes, and other backward classes. Reservation for the other classes could be provided under Article 16(1) and not to scheduled tribes to whom the reservation had been provided under Article 16(4). Thus, as argued on behalf of Respondents, it could not be said to be a case of classification made under Article 16(1) of the Constitution of India. It was a case of tinkering with the percentage of reservation permissible as per the dictum of Indra Sawhney. Other incumbents who were in the reserved classes such as scheduled castes and other backward classes and even Scheduled Tribes who had settled after prescribed date beside incumbents of open category, were deprived of the right to stake claim to obtain public employment as against the posts in question. In the background of the discussion made in the earlier part of the judgment, it was crystal clear that the order passed providing hundred reservation was arbitrary, illegal, impermissible, and unconstitutional.

xi. The G.O. in question requires candidate or the parents to reside in the area. There was no rhyme or reason to require continuous residence for last fifty years or more. It overlooks the rights of various other persons who might have settled decades together in the area in question. It was discriminatory vis-C -vis to the scheduled tribes also settled in the area and it had no purpose to be achieved and imposes restriction which was not even provided in the Presidential Order issued under Article 371D of the Constitution of India with respect to residential or educational requirements. Thus, it did not lay down valid conditions. The same was fixed in highly unreasonable and arbitrary manner and limits zone of consideration to miniscule where an opportunity for public employment has to be afforded to all concerned with reasonable rights.

ppp

THREE

SAURAV YADAV AND ORS. VS. STATE OF UTTAR PRADESH AND ORS., 2020

Hon'ble Judges/Coram:

U.U. Lalit and S. Ravindra Bhat and Hrishikesh Roy, JJ.

Equivalent Citation: 2021(1)ADJ201, AIR2021SC233, 2021(2) ALJ 18, 2021 2 AWC1149SC, 2021(1)ESC206(SC), 2021LabIC461, (2021)1MLJ390, (2021)4SCC542, 2021 (1) SCJ 202, 2021(1)SCT87(SC), 2021(3)SLR298(SC), MANU/SC/0960/2020

Relevant sections: Article 16(1) of Constitution of India

Number of pages in original Judgment: 35

Case Note:

Service - Women candidate - Filing of quota - Applicant had participated in Selection Process initiated for filling up posts of Constables in U.P. Police and secured marks - They had applied in categories of OBC-Female and SC-Female - Their claim had been rejected by State Government - Hence, present application - Whether State had erred in not considering claim of OBC female and SC female candidates against posts meant for General Category female candidates.

Brief Facts:

The Applicants had participated in the Selection Process initiated for filling up posts of Constables in U.P. Police and secured marks. They had applied in the categories of OBC-Female and SC-Female respectively. State had not considered the claim of OBC female and SC female candidates against the posts meant for General Category female candidates.

Held, while partly allowing the application:
U.U. Lalit, J.

i. The High Courts of Rajasthan, Bombay, Uttarakhand, and Gujarat had adopted the same principle while dealing with horizontal reservation whereas the High Court of Allahabad and Madhya Pradesh had taken a contrary view. These two views, for facility, were referred to as the first view and the second view respectively. The second view that weighed with the High Courts of Allahabad and Madhya Pradesh was essentially based on the premise that after the first two steps as detailed in the decision in Anil Kumar Gupta and Ors. and after vertical reservations are provided for, at the stage of accommodating candidates for effecting horizontal reservation, the candidates from reserved categories can be adjusted only against their own categories under the concerned vertical reservation and not against the Open or General Category.

ii. The second view would thus not only lead to irrational results where more meritorious candidates may possibly get sidelined as indicated above but will, of necessity, result in acceptance of a postulate that Open/ General seats are reserved for candidates other than those coming from vertical reservation categories. Such view will be completely opposed to the long line of decisions of this Court.

iii. The Appellant No. 1 and similarly situated candidates had secured more marks than the last candidates selected in Open/General Category, the logical consequence must be to annul said selection and direct the authorities to do the exercise de novo. However, considering the facts that those selected candidates had actually undergone training and are presently in employment and that there were adequate number of vacancies available, this court mould the relief and direct that all candidates coming from OBC Female Category who had secured more marks than the marks secured by the last candidate appointed in General Category-Female must be offered employment as Constables in Uttar Pradesh Police.

S. Ravindra Bhat, J.

i.   As was apparent from a plain reading of the government order, the only stipulation with respect to treatment of horizontal reservation for women, was that in case a woman candidate was selected, she would be adjusted against the appropriate social category she belongs to (SC/ST/OBC/OC). However, there was no rule, or direction which prohibits the adjustment of socially reserved categories of women in the general category or open category.

ii. The open category was not a quota, but rather available to all women and men alike. Similarly, as held in Rajesh Kumar Dari, there is no quota for men. If this court was to accept the second view (as held in Ajay Kumar v. State of UP and in State of Madhya Pradesh and Anr. v. Uday Sisode and Ors.), the result would be confining the number of women candidates, irrespective of their performance, in their social reservation categories and therefore, destructive of logic and merit. The second view, therefore-perhaps unconsciously supports-but definitely results in confining the number of women in the select list to the overall numerical quota assured by the rule.

iii. The second view collapse completely, when more than the stipulated percentage twenty percent of women candidates figure in the most meritorious category. The said second view in Ajay Kumar and Uday Sisode thus penalizes merit. The principle of mobility or migration, upheld by this Court in Union of India v. Ramesh Ram and other cases, would then have discriminatory application, as it would apply for mobility of special category men, but would not apply to the case of women in such special categories to women who score equal to or more than their counterparts in the open/general category.

iv. It was too late in the day for the Respondent state to contend that women candidates who were entitled to benefit of social category reservations, cannot fill open category vacancies. The said view was starkly exposed as misconceived, because it would result in such women candidates with less merit (in the open category) being selected, and those with more merit than such selected candidates, (in the social/vertical reservation category) being left out of selection.

❦❦❦

FOUR

Tamil Nadu Medical Officers Association and Ors. Vs. Union of India (UOI) and Ors., 2020

Hon'ble Judges/Coram:

Arun Mishra, Indira Banerjee, Vineet Saran, M.R. Shah and Aniruddha Bose, JJ.

Equivalent Citation: 2020(3)ESC703(SC), 2020(4)J.L.J.R.415, (2020)7MLJ564, 2020(4)PLJR392, (2021)6SCC568, 2020(3)SCT336(SC), MANU/SC/0662/2020

Relevant sections: Regulations 9, 9(IV) and 9(VII) of MCI Postgraduate Medical Education Regulations, 2000

Number of pages in original Judgment: 74

Case Note:

Education - In service doctors - Reservation thereto - Regulations 9, 9(IV) and 9(VII) of MCI Postgraduate Medical Education Regulations, 2000 - Present petitions filed to declare that Regulation 9 of Education Regulations, 2000, more particularly, Regulation 9(IV) and 9(VII), did not take away power of States under Entry 25, List III to provide for separate source of entry for in-service candidates seeking admission to Degree courses - Whether State had legislative competence and/or authority to provide for separate source of entry for in-service candidates seeking admission to postgraduate degree/diploma courses, in exercise of powers under Entry 25, List III.

Brief Facts:

The present writ petition filed to declare by issuance of a writ of mandamus or any other suitable writ/order/direction that Regulation 9 of the Post Graduate Medical Education Regulations, 2000 more particularly, Regulation 9(IV) and 9(VII), did not take away the power of the States under Entry 25, List III to provide for a separate source of entry for in-service candidates seeking admission to Degree courses. Alternatively, if Regulation 9 of the Post Graduate Medical Education Regulations, 2000 was understood to now allow for States to provide for a separate source of entry for in-service candidates seeking admission to Degree courses, declare, by issuance of a writ of mandamus or any other suitable writ/order/direction, Regulation 9, more particularly, Regulation 9(IV) and 9(VII) as being arbitrary, discriminatory and violative of Article 14 and 19(1)(g) of the Constitution and also ultra vires the provisions of the Indian Medical Council Act, 1956.

Held, while allowing the petitions:

i. Entry 66 List I was a specific entry having a very limited scope.

ii. It deals with coordination and determination of standards in higher education.

iii. The words coordination and determination of standards would mean laying down the said standards.

iv. The Medical Council of India which has been constituted under the provisions of the Indian Medical Council Act, 1956 is the creature of the statute in exercise of powers under Entry 66 List I and had no power to make any provision for reservation, more particularly, for in-service candidates by the concerned States, in exercise of powers under Entry 25 List III.

v. Regulation 9 of MCI Regulations, 2000 did not deal with and/or make provisions for reservation and/or affect the legislative competence and authority of the concerned States to make reservation and/or make special provision like the provision providing for a separate source of entry for in-service candidates seeking admission to postgraduate degree courses and therefore the concerned States to be within their authority and/or legislative competence to provide for a separate source of entry for in-service candidates seeking admission to postgraduate degree courses in exercise of powers under Entry 25 of List III.

vi. If it was held that Regulation 9, more particularly, Regulation 9(IV) deals with reservation for in-service candidates, in that case, it would be ultra vires of the Indian Medical Council Act, 1956 and it would be beyond the legislative competence under Entry 66 List I.

vii. Regulation 9 of MCI Regulations, 2000 to the extent tinkering with reservation provided by the State for in-service candidates was ultra vires on the ground that it was arbitrary, discriminatory and violative of Articles 14 and 21 of the Constitution of India.

viii. The State had the legislative competence and/or authority to provide for a separate source of entry for in-service candidates seeking admission to postgraduate degree/diploma courses, in exercise of powers under Entry 25, List III. However, it was observed that policy must provide that subsequent to obtaining the postgraduate degree by the concerned in-service doctors obtaining entry in degree courses through such separate channel serve the State in the rural, tribal and hilly areas at least for five years after obtaining the degree/diploma and for that they will execute bonds for such sum the respective States may consider fit and proper.

ix. It was specifically observed and clarified that the present decision shall operate prospectively and any admissions given earlier taking a contrary view shall not be affected by this judgment.

Aniruddha Bose, J.

i. The admission process stipulating a distinct source of entry for in-service candidates by itself would not constitute breach of the provisions of Clause 9 of the 2000 Regulations, provided that the minimum standards mandated by the said Regulations for being eligible to pursue postgraduate medical degree course were adhered to. A separate source of entry for in-service doctors through the State merit list would come within the legislative power and competence of the State. The reservation for in-service doctors had been a long standing practise and the rationale behind such reservation appears to be reasonable. But this court refrain from dilating on the necessity of maintaining such practise as in this judgment, we are primarily concerned with the question of competence of State authorities in making Rules providing for such reservation.

ii. Clause 9(4) of the 2000 Regulations stipulates entry into the postgraduate courses from the two merit lists, one all India and the other that of the State. The same was the scheme of Clause 9(IV) in its erstwhile form. The dispute in these proceedings, however, was mainly on admission norms to postgraduate degree courses. If the State authorities provide reservation for in-service doctors from within the State's own merit list, was that such an exercise would be relatable to the admission process and the same would not be in breach of any prohibition flowing from the 2000 Regulations. This would entail some form of variation of the merit list of the State, but we do not find any prohibition under the 2000 Regulations against a State undertaking that exercise. Such step undertaken by the State would be relatable to the State's legislative power derived from Entry 25 of the Concurrent List and not covered by the 2000 Regulations. There was no repugnancy with the 2000 Regulations if the State authorities create such a distinct channel of entry.

iii. There was no bar in Clause 9 of the Postgraduate Medical Education Regulations, 2000 as it prevailed and subsequently amended on individual States in providing for reservation of in-service doctors for admission into postgraduate medical degree courses. But to take benefit of such separate entry channel, the aspiring in-service doctors must clear the NEET Examination with the minimum prescribed marks as stipulated in the 2000 Regulations. This court respectfully differ from the views expressed by the Bench of this Court in the case of the State of Uttar Pradesh and Ors. v. Dinesh Singh Chauhan to the extent it has been held in the said decision that reservation for the said category of in-service doctors by the State would be contrary to the provisions of 2000 Regulations. That was not the correct view under the Constitution. The reference was answered accordingly.

ϼϼϼ

FIVE

DIRECTOR TRANSPORT DEPARTMENT, UNION TERRITORY ADMINISTRATION OF DADRA AND NAGAR HAVELI SILVASSA AND ORS. VS. ABHINAV DIPAKBHAI PATEL, 2019

Hon'ble Judges/Coram:

L. Nageswara Rao and M.R. Shah, JJ.

Equivalent Citation: 2019(4)ALLMR433, 2019(5)BomCR103, 2019(2)ESC458(SC), 2019(7)SCALE590, (2019)6SCC434, 2019 (7) SCJ 507, 2019(3)SCT112(SC), 2019(2)SLJ72(SC), 2019(6)SLR136(SC), MANU/SC/0704/2019

Relevant sections: Articles 341(1) and 342(1) of the Constitution of India

Number of pages in original Judgment: 06

Case Note:

Service - Appointment - Eligibility - Judgment of High Court directing appointment of Respondent as Assistant Motor Vehicle Inspector by allowing his Writ Petition was subject matter of Appeal - Whether benefit of reservation could only be claimed by a person who was domiciled in the Union Territory.

Brief Facts:

Respondent belongs to "Dhodia" caste which is recognized as a Scheduled Tribe category in the State of Gujarat as well as in the Union Territory of Dadra and Nagar Haveli. He holds a caste certificate which was issued by the concerned competent authority in the State of Gujarat. He shifted his residence from Gujarat to the Union Territory of Dadra and Nagar Haveli. He owns a residential accommodation in the Union Territory and has a Voter's I.D. card to show that he was a resident of Dadra and Nagar Haveli. An advertisement was issued calling for applications for filling up two posts of Assistant Motor Vehicle Inspectors, one of them reserved for the Scheduled Tribe category. Ministry of Home Affairs, clarified that, the Respondent was eligible for appointment and advised the concerned authority to take appropriate action as per the directions issued by the National Commission for Schedule Tribes. An order was passed by the National Commission directing the Appellants to issue a letter of appointment in favour of the Respondent. Since no action was taken to appoint the Respondent, he was constrained to file a Writ Petition in the High Court. High Court held that, Respondent was found to be a resident of the Union Territory of Dadra and Nagar Haveli and though he migrated from the State of Gujarat, he was entitled to be considered for appointment as a reserved category candidate. On the basis of the said findings, the High Court directed the Appellants to appoint Respondent as Assistant Motor Vehicle Inspector with effect from the date of appointment of other candidates from the same selection process. Appellants referred to various circulars which indicate the policy of the Union Territory that the reservation was applicable only to the locals and not to the migrants. He argued that the benefit of reservation can only be claimed by a person who is domiciled in the Union Territory.

Held, while dismissing the appeal:

i. A person belonging to a Scheduled Caste or a Scheduled Tribe which is notified by the President for a Union Territory is entitled to be considered as a reserved candidate provided he is a resident of the said

Union Territory.

ii. There is no dispute that, the Respondent was a resident in the Union Territory of Dadra and Nagar Haveli for six years prior to the date of advertisement. He stated in the Writ Petition that he owns an apartment in which he was residing and he married a woman from "Dhodia" tribe in the Union Territory. He further stated that his name is in the Voter's List in the Union Territory. These facts have not been disputed by the Appellants. The Presidential Notification issued for the Union Territory of Dadra and Nagar Haveli extends the benefit of reservation to the Scheduled Tribes mentioned therein on the basis of residence and not on the basis of origin. Gross injustice is caused to the Respondent by the action of the Appellants in not appointing him in spite of the advice of the Union of India and the direction issued by the National Commission for Scheduled Tribes. The appointment of Respondent as Assistant Motor Vehicle Inspector does not brook any further delay.

iii. No reason to interfere with judgment of High Court. Appeal dismissed.

ϸϸϸ

SIX

SANJAI KUMAR AND ORS. VS. PRABHAT KUMAR AND ORS., 2019

Hon'ble Judges/Coram:
U.U. Lalit and M.R. Shah, JJ.

Equivalent Citation: 2021(1)ESC339(SC), 2019(17)SCALE778, (2020)3SCC184, (2020)1SCC(LS)483, 2020(1)SCT459(SC), 2020(3)SLR484(SC), MANU/SC/1732/2019

Relevant sections: Section 23 of the RTE Act; Sections 12 and 12A of the NCTE Act

Number of pages in original Judgment: 11

Case Note:

Contempt of Court - Selection process - Obedience of order - Present contempt petitions filed against order by which this court directed State to fill up the vacancies of Assistant Teachers in schools pursuant to advertisement - Further, it was also directed that State Government shall appoint candidates, whose names had not been weeded out in malpractice and who have obtained/secured seventy percent marks in the Teacher Eligibility Test (TET) and candidates belonging to Scheduled Caste/ Scheduled Tribe/Other Backward Classes and physically handicapped persons, shall be appointed if they had obtained/secured sixty-five percent marks - Petitioner submitted that in terms of interim orders issued by this Court, State did not appoint Contempt Petitioners and as such orders passed by this Court were violated - Whether there was anything wrong in process undertaken by State Government in pursuance of various interim orders passed by this Court and there was any violation of any of orders passed by this Court.

Brief Facts:

The present contempt petition filed direct the State to fill up the vacancies of Assistant Teachers in the schools pursuant to the advertisement and further direct that the State Government shall appoint the candidates, whose names had not been weeded out in the malpractice and who had obtained/secured seventy percent marks in the Teacher Eligibility Test (TET). The candidates belonging to Scheduled Caste/ Scheduled Tribe/Other Backward Classes and the physically handicapped persons, shall be appointed if they have obtained/secured sixty-five percent marks. It was submitted by the Petitioners inter alia that the State did not appoint the Contempt Petitioners and as such the orders passed by this Court were violated.

Held, while dismissing the petitions:

i. The following facts emerged from record:

a. The large number of vacancies were lying unfilled while the Civil Appeals were pending in this Court. Taking into account the interest of the student community those appointments were required to be made. A principle was, therefore adopted by order that those who had obtained more than seventy marks in TET Examination from the general category and those who had obtained more than sixty five marks from the reserved categories be given appointments. The idea was clear that such candidates would normally stand selected in the ultimate process of selection. It was, however, made clear that such appointments would not entitle the selected candidates to raise any claim in equity.

b. In the selection process undertaken thereafter, initially candidates were selected and a direction was issued to fill up those posts.

c. The next order recorded that as against certain posts which were advertised, certain candidates were appointed, who after completion of training were actually working while candidates were undergoing training, leaving certain posts still vacant.

d. The exercise of selecting those who had secured minimum marks in terms of criteria devised by order also resulted in finding persons eligible subject to verification of antecedents, as was recorded in the order.

e. The list of candidates was published and it was a matter of record that the names of the contempt Petitioners were part of this list.

f. According to the Affidavit out of these candidates, only certain candidates could be appointed as the others either did not take part in the selection process or had not opted for certain Districts or could not be selected going by the cut-off for the concerned District. This development had happened way back and the affidavit was on record since then.

g. The State thereafter published another advertisement so that if any candidate was left out, his candidature could be considered. Steps were thereafter taken and another advertisement was published. The Affidavit as quoted in the order, dealt with this issue in clear terms and was thus part of the record.

h. The Affidavit thus made it clear that as on the date when the affidavit was filed, certain vacancies were filled up and appointment letters were being issued in addition. It was also stated that candidates were given ad-hoc appointments in terms of the order and were not included in the number.

Thus, the reasons for not appointing all the persons who were part of list of candidates were available on record.

a. At no stage any grievance was made till the matter was disposed of which gave the status of permanency to those who were appointed under various interim orders passed by this Court.

j. The grievance was made for the first time almost a year after when these contempt petitions were filed.

k. The order had, therefore, observed that the Court could not disregard the fact that challenge had been raised more than a year after the final Judgment. Even then, the State Government was called upon to indicate on affidavit certain issues. The reason was obvious that if there was large scale infraction of interim orders passed by this Court which merged in the final Judgment, the matter could still have been considered.

i. However, the response filed by the State Government now indicates with clarity that no fresh appointments were effected and no person other than those who satisfied the requirements laid down by this Court in its Order as modified by further orders, was given any appointment. The

State Government had also placed on record the District wise break-up of all candidates appointed in various categories in all Districts of the State. Even after the filing of the response by the State, nothing substantial cold be pointed out by any of the candidates or contempt Petitioners.

ii. Therefore, there was nothing wrong in the process undertaken by the State Government in pursuance of various interim orders passed by this Court and also in pursuance of the judgment and final order. The fact that out of candidates only few could be selected and the reasons for non-selection of rest of the candidates, were part of the record. In any case, response filed by the State was also clear. In the totality of the circumstances, there had not been any violation of any of the orders passed by this Court as alleged in the contempt petitions or otherwise.

ᗡᗡᗡ

SEVEN

ANUPAL SINGH AND ORS. VS. STATE OF U.P. AND ORS., 2019

Hon'ble Judges/Coram:

R. Banumathi and A.S. Bopanna, JJ.

Equivalent Citation: AIR2019SC5652, 2019(6)BLJ90, 2019(4)ESC912(SC), 2020LabIC497, 2019(13)SCALE216, (2020)2SCC173, (2020)1SCC(LS)191, 2020(1)SLJ435(SC), 2020(4)SLR270(SC), MANU/SC/1349/2019

Relevant sections: Rule 15 and Rule 6 of UP Subordinate Agriculture Services Rules, 1993;

Number of pages in original Judgment: 25

Case Note:

Service - Selection process - Revising of vacancies - Commission issued advertisement inviting applications for post of Subordinate Agriculture Services, Cadre-III (Technical Assistant Group-C) - State Government approved revised vacancies for different categories of persons - Based upon revised requisition, Commission declared result of written examination - After declaration of result of written examination, Commission issued Office Memorandum notifying posts for Unreserved/General category, SC category, ST category and OBC category - Finally, when result of select list candidates was declared, private Respondents did not qualify - Writ petitions came to be filed before High Court assailing validity of Office Memorandum and result declared praying that they be quashed - High Court while upholding result of written examination, quashed selection process subsequent to written examination - Hence, present appeal - Whether High Court erred in quashing selection process subsequent to written examination while upholding result of written examination.

Brief Facts:

The Commission issued an advertisement inviting applications for 6628 vacancies of Subordinate Agriculture Services, Cadre-III (Technical Assistant Group-C). The State Government approved the revised vacancies for different categories of persons in accordance with the applicable reservation Rules and accordingly, revised the requisition. Based upon the revised requisition, Commission declared the result of the written examination wherein, both the Appellants as well as the private Respondents were declared successful. After declaration of the result of written examination, the Commission issued an Office Memorandum notifying posts for Unreserved/General category, SC category, ST category and OBC category. The successful candidates who cleared the written examination appeared for interview. Finally, when the result of select list candidates was declared, the private Respondents did not qualify. Number of writ petitions came to be filed before the High Court by the unsuccessful candidates against Respondents No. 1 to 4 and by impleading some of the successful candidates assailing the validity of the Office Memorandum and the result declared praying that they be quashed. The High Court while upholding the result of written examination for the post of Technical Assistant-Group-C Agriculture Department, quashed selection process subsequent to the written examination and directed the Principal Secretary, to send requisition to the Commission on the basis of quantifiable data and cadre strength as well as actual persons working in different categories so that the interview may be conducted afresh and complete the selection.

Held, while allowing the appeal:

The Office Memorandum issued by the Commission revising the number of vacancies was based upon the revised requisition of the Government. The revised requisition of the Government was only to rectify the wrongful calculation of the number of vacancies in different categories and to comply with the requisite percentage of quota of reservation in different categories as per Uttar Pradesh Public Services (Reservation for Scheduled Castes, Scheduled Tribes and Other Backward Classes) Act, 1994. In view of Rule 15 and Rule 6 of UP Subordinate Agriculture Services Rules, 1993 (Agriculture Service Rules, 1993), the Recruitment Authority was empowered to rectify the wrongful calculation and make a revised requisition of number of vacancies in different categories which is in accordance with the provisions of UP Reservation Act, 1994 and Agriculture Service Rules, 1993. Absorption of diploma holders were required to be done only against the General quota. The High Court was not right in saying that the diploma holders ought not to have been absorbed against the General category so as to alter the advertised number of posts against the General category. Revising the number of vacancies in different categories to satisfy the statutory requirement of reservation quota as per UP Reservation Act, 1994 and this would not amount to changing the Rules of the game after the commencement of the selection process. Having participated in the interview and when they failed in the final selection, it was not open to the private Respondents/intervenors to turn around and challenge the revised notification and the final select list. The filling up of the unfilled horizontal reservation by the candidates from the respective vertical reservation was in accordance with the policy of the government and the same cannot be faulted with. The candidates were not issued the appointment orders in order to keep the appointment within the permissible percentage of reservation as per UP Reservation Act, 1994. The power under Article 142 of the Constitution of India could not be exercised to issue direction to the first Respondent-State to issue appointment orders to candidates.

ᐅᐅᐅ

EIGHT

B.K. PAVITRA AND ORS. VS. THE UNION OF INDIA (UOI) AND ORS., 2019

Hon'ble Judges/Coram:

U.U. Lalit and Dr. D.Y. Chandrachud, JJ.

Equivalent Citation: AIR2019SC2723, 2019(4) AKR 258, 2019(4)ALT74, 2019(2)ESC495(SC), ILR 2019 4411, 2019(4)KarLJ1, 2019LabIC4074, 2019(8)SCALE205, (2019)16SCC129, 2019 (10) SCJ 1, 2019(2)SLJ198(SC), MANU/SC/0738/2019

Relevant sections: Articles 14 and 16 of Constitution of India, 1950; Sections 3 and 4 of Karnataka Extension of Consequential Seniority to Government Servants Promoted on Basis of Reservation (to Posts in Civil Services of the State) Act, 2018

Number of pages in original Judgment: 60

Case Note:

Service - Benefit of Consequential Seniority - Validity of Reservation Act - Sections 3 and 4 of Karnataka Extension of Consequential Seniority to Government Servants Promoted on Basis of Reservation (to Posts in Civil Services of the State) Act, 2018 (Reservation Act, 2018) and Articles 14 and 16 of Constitution of India, 1950 - Principal challenge in present batch of cases was to validity of Reservation Act, 2018 - Whether Reservation Act, 2018 had cured deficiency which was noticed by B.K. Pavitra I in respect of

Reservation Act, 2002.

Brief Facts:

Challenge in present cases is to the validity of Reservation Act, 2018. The enactment provides, among other things, for consequential seniority to persons belonging to the Scheduled Castes and Scheduled Tribes promoted under the reservation policy of the State of Karnataka. The law protects consequential seniority from 24 April 1978. The Reservation Act, 2018 was preceded in time by the Karnataka Determination of Seniority of the Government Servants Promoted on the Basis of the Reservation (to the Posts in the Civil Services of the State) Act 2002. The constitutional validity of the Reservation Act, 2002 was challenged in B.K. Pavitra v. Union of India. A two judge Bench of this Court held Sections 3 and 4 of the Reservation Act 2002 to be ultra vires of Articles 14 and 16 of the Constitution on the ground that, an exercise for determining "inadequacy of representation", "backwardness" and the impact on "overall efficiency" had not preceded the enactment of the law. Such an exercise was held to be mandated by the decision of a Constitution Bench of this Court in M. Nagaraj v. Union of India. In the absence of the State of Karnataka having collected quantifiable data on the above three parameters, the Reservation Act, 2002 was held to be invalid. The legislature in the State of Karnataka enacted the Reservation Act, 2018 after this Court invalidated the Reservation Act, 2002 in B.K. Pavitra I. The grievance of the Petitioners is that, the state legislature has virtually re-enacted the earlier legislation without curing its defects. According to the Petitioners, it is not open to a legislative body governed by the parameters of a written constitution to override a judicial decision, without taking away its basis. On the other hand, the State government has asserted that, an exercise for collecting "quantifiable data" was in fact carried out, consistent with the parameters required by the decision in Nagaraj. The Petitioners question both the process and the outcome of the exercise carried out by the state for collecting quantifiable data. Karnataka government argued that, the state legislature is competent to enact a law with retrospective or retroactive operation. It was further stated that, the legislative competence of the state legislature to enact law is traceable to Article 16 (4A) and merely because the legislation confers seniority with effect from 1978, will not lead to its invalidation.

Held, while dismissing the appeal:

i. The decision in B.K. Pavitra I was rendered on 9 February 2017. The Ratna Prabha Committee was established on 22 March 2017. Its report was examined by a Cabinet Sub-Committee on 4 August 2017 and was eventually approved by the Cabinet on 7 August 2017. The Ratna Prabha Committee report was commissioned to: (i) collect information on cadre wise representation of SC and ST employees in all government departments; (ii) collect information on backwardness of SCs and STs; and (iii) study the effect on the administration due to the promotion of SCs and STs.

ii. Once an opinion has been formed by the State government on the basis of the report submitted by an expert committee which collected, collated and analysed relevant data, it is impossible for the Court to hold that, the compelling reasons which Nagaraj requires the State to demonstrate have not been established. Even if there were to be some errors in data collection, that will not justify the invalidation of a law which the competent legislature was within its power to enact. After the decision in B.K. Pavitra I, the Ratna Prabha Committee was correctly appointed to carry out the required exercise. Once that exercise has been carried out, the Court must be circumspect in exercising the power of judicial review to re-evaluate the factual material on record.

iii. The challenge in the present case is to the validity of the Reservation Act, 2018 which provides for consequential seniority. In other words, the nature or extent of reservation granted to the SCs and STs at the entry level in appointment is not under challenge. The Reservation Act, 2018 adopts the principle that consequential seniority is not an additional benefit but a consequence of the promotion which is granted to the SCs and STs. In protecting consequential seniority as an incident of promotion, the Reservation Act, 2018 constitutes an exercise of the enabling power conferred by Article 16 (4A). The concept of creamy layer has no relevance to the grant of consequential seniority. There is merit in the submission of the State of Karnataka that, progression in a cadre based on promotion cannot be treated as the acquisition of creamy layer status. The decision in Jarnail rejected the submission that a member of an SC or ST who reaches a higher post no longer has a taint of untouchability or backwardness.

iv. In sustaining the validity of Articles 16 (4A) and 16 (4B) against a challenge of violating the basic structure, Nagaraj applied the test of width and the test of identity. The Constitution Bench ruled that, the catch-up Rule and consequential seniority are not constitutional requirements. They were held not to be implicit in Clauses (1) to (4) of Article 16. Nagaraj held that they are not constitutional limitations or principles but are concepts derived from service jurisprudence. Hence, neither the obliteration of those concepts nor their insertion would violate the equality code contained in Articles 14, 15 and 16. The principle postulated in Nagaraj is that consequential seniority is a concept purely based in service jurisprudence. The incorporation of consequential seniority would hence not violate the constitutional mandate of equality. This being the true constitutional position, the protection of consequential seniority as an incident of promotion does not require the application of the creamy layer test. Articles 16 (4A) and 16 (4B) were held to not obliterate any of the constitutional limitations and to fulfil the width test. In the above view of the matter, it is evident that the concept of creamy layer has no application in assessing the validity of the Reservation Act 2018 which is designed to protect consequential seniority upon promotion of persons belonging to the SCs and STs.

v. Sections 3 and 4 of the Reservation Act, 2018 came into force on 17 June 1995. The other provisions came into force "at once" as provided in Section 1(2). Section 4 stipulates that, the consequential seniority already granted to government servants belonging to the SCs and STs in accordance with the reservation order with effect from 27 April 1978 shall be valid and shall be protected.

vi. Since promotions granted prior to 1 March 1996 were protected, it was logical for the legislature to protect consequential seniority. The object of the Reservation Act, 2018 is to accord consequential seniority to promotees against roster points. In this view of the matter, we find no reason to hold that the provisions in regard to retrospectivity in the Ratna Prabha Committee report are either arbitrary or unconstitutional.

vii. The benefit of consequential seniority has been extended from the date of the Reservation Order 1978 under which promotions based on reservation were accorded.

viii. The Ratna Prabha Committee collected data from thirty one departments of the State Government of Karnataka. It has been pointed out on behalf of the State that corporations such as KPTCL and other public sector undertakings fall within the administrative control of one of the departments of the State government. The position in thirty one departments was taken as representative of the position in public employment under the State. The over representation in KPTCL and PWD has been projected by the Petitioners with reference to the total number of posts which have been filled. On the other hand, the quota is fixed and the roster applies as regards the total sanctioned posts as held in Sabharwal and Nagaraj. On the contrary, the data submitted by the State of Karnataka indicates that if consequential seniority is not allowed, there would be under representation of the reserved categories. Finally, under the Government Order dated 13 April 1999, reservation in promotion in favour of SC's and ST's has been provided until the representation for these categories reaches 15 per cent and 3 per cent, respectively. The State has informed the Court that the above Government Order is applicable to KPTCL and PWD, as well.

ix. The challenge to the constitutional validity of the Reservation Act 2018 is lacking in substance. Following the decision in B.K. Pavitra I, the State government duly carried out the exercise of collating and analysing data on the compelling factors adverted to by the Constitution Bench in Nagaraj. The Reservation Act, 2018 has cured the deficiency which was noticed by B.K. Pavitra I in respect of the Reservation Act, 2002. The Reservation Act 2018 does not amount to a usurpation of judicial power by the state legislature. It is Nagaraj and Jarnail compliant. The Reservation Act, 2018 is a valid exercise of the enabling power conferred by Article 16 (4A) of the Constitution.

x. The constitutional validity of the Reservation Act, 2018 has been upheld. Accordingly, the review petitions and miscellaneous applications shall also stand dismissed in view of the judgment in the present case.

ᭇᭇᭇ

NINE

GOVT. OF NCT DELHI AND ORS. VS. PRADEEP KUMAR AND ORS., 2019

Hon'ble Judges/Coram:

R. Banumathi, A.S. Bopanna and Hrishikesh Roy, JJ.

Equivalent Citation: 263(2019)DLT633, 2020(1)ESC1(SC), [2020(165)FLR385], 2019(4)J.L.J.R.484, 2019(4)PLJR442, 2019(14)SCALE371, (2019)10SCC120, (2019)2SCC(LS)771, 2020(1)SLJ119(SC), 2020(5)SLR264(SC), MANU/SC/1466/2019

Relevant sections:

Number of pages in original Judgment: 08

Case Note:

Education - Eligibility - Lack of - Advertisement was issued by Delhi Subordinate Services Selection Board where, for vacancies of Special Education Teachers - Candidature of Respondents were held to be not-eligible on ground that applicants were CTET qualified as OBC but OBC outsider - Aggrieved by decision of Selection Board, Respondents filed application before Tribunal - Tribunal took view that there shall be no bar in considering meritorious applicants in unreserved category if no weightage was given to CTET marks in preparation of final merit list - Consequential direction was issued to authorities for appointment of Original Applicants - Against said order, writ petition was filed before High Court - High Court held that as performance of Respondents were more meritorious than others selected in unreserved category, Tribunal's decision in favour of

Respondents was upheld - Hence, present appeal - Whether Respondents who had secured CTET qualification form outside Delhi as OBC candidate by availing five percent relaxation in qualifying marks be considered for employment against post of Special Education Teacher in Government of NCT, Delhi.

Brief Facts:

The Advertisement was issued by the Delhi Sub-ordinate Services Selection Board where, for the vacancies of Special Education Teachers. Respondents offered their candidature for the vacancies in Delhi and appeared in the recruitment test. But their candidature were held to be not-eligible, through the office order on ground that the applicants were CTET qualified as OBC but OBC outsider. Aggrieved by the above decision of the Selection Board, the Original Applicants filed the application before Tribunal. The Tribunal considered the rival contention and observed that rejection of the candidature of the Original Applicants would mean that the Appellants do not recognize the CTET qualification. The Tribunal took the view that there shall be no bar in considering meritorious applicants in the unreserved category if no weightage was given to CTET marks in preparation of the final merit list. Consequential direction was issued to the authorities for appointment of Original Applicants, in terms of their respective position in the merit list. On writ petition against said order, the High Court accordingly held that once the candidate had obtained the CTET qualification, the marks secured in the qualification examination is immaterial for consideration of their candidature, for the unreserved category vacancies. As the performance of the Respondents were more meritorious than others selected in the unreserved category, the Tribunal's decision in favour of the Respondents was upheld.

Held, while allowing the appeal:

i. The Respondents were competing for general category vacancies. All others in this group had obtained their CTET eligibility qualification, securing the normal pass marks without availing any relaxation of pass norms. On the other hand, the Respondents despite their lesser marks in the CTET examination, could qualify only because they availed the relaxation benefits as OBC category examinees. Their eligibility qualification is secured under relaxed norms meant for OBC category and therefore this court did not think it is proper to consider them to be eligible for the general category vacancies and contention to the contrary was unacceptable.

ii. The Respondents with their CTET qualification under relaxed norms would be eligible for OBC category posts provided their OBC status was certified and recognized by the Delhi government. But such not being the case, they were ineligible for the reserved category vacancies. To allow them to migrate and compete for the open category vacancies would not be permissible simply because, they had secured the CTET qualification with relaxation of pass marks meant for those belonging to the OBC category. As the Respondents had not secured the normal pass marks for general category, their eligibility for the general category vacancies was not secured. Therefore, their performance in the selection examination would be of no relevance, in the present process.

iii. As earlier discussed, this case concerns qualifications obtained with concession in pass marks. Such concession would have a direct impact on standards of competence and merit in the recruitment of Special Education Teachers. The principles of reservation under the Constitution of India are intended to be confined to a specifically earmarked category and the unreserved category must be protected, to avoid dilution of competence and merit. If Vikas Sankhala case was interpreted shorn of its peculiar facts, as had been suggested by the Respondents' counsel, it would in perception, considering that Respondents secured the qualification under relaxed norms, would lead to dilution of merit in the unreserved category. The arguments made to the contrary by the Respondents was therefore rejected.

ppp

TEN

Niravkumar Dilipbhai Makwana Vs. Gujarat Public Service Commission and Ors., 2019

Hon'ble Judges/Coram:

S. Abdul Nazeer and Indira Banerjee, JJ.

Equivalent Citation: AIR2019SC3149, 2019(6)ALT135, 2019 5 AWC4637SC, 128(2019)CLT527, 2019(3)ESC686(SC), 2019(4)J.L.J.R.10, 2019LabIC3136, 2020(3)LLN569(SC), 2019(II)OLR241, 2019(4)PLJR48, 2019(4)RLW2908(SC), 2019(9)SCALE17, (2019)7SCC383, (2019)2SCC(LS)337, 2019 (10) SCJ 600, 2019(3)SCT359(SC), 2019(2)SLJ463(SC), 2019(5)SLR198(SC), 2019(4)SLR507(SC), (2019)5WBLR(SC)438, MANU/SC/0880/2019

Relevant sections: Article 16(4) of the Constitution of India, 1950

Number of pages in original Judgment: 08

Ratio Decidendi:

It is purely a matter of discretion of State Government to formulate a policy for concession, exemption, preference or relaxation either conditionally or unconditionally in favour of backward classes of citizens

Case Note:

Service - General category seats - Migration thereto - Article 16(4) of the Constitution of India, 1950- Appeal was against impugned order of High Court observing that, all those candidates belonging to a reserved category, if they avail the benefit of age relaxation, same was to be considered as relaxation in standard and therefore, such candidates who got benefit of age relaxation were not entitled to be considered in general category - Whether a candidate who had availed of an age relaxation in a selection process as a result of belonging to a reserved category, could thereafter seek to be accommodated in/or migrated to general category seat.

Brief Facts:

Gujarat (GPSC) had issued an advertisement and corrigendum thereafter for 47 posts of Assistant Conservator of Forests ('ACF') (Class-II) and 120 posts of Range Forest Officer ('RFO') (Class-II). The Appellant submitted an application in the category of SEBC. He successfully passed the examination conducted by GPSC. It is the case of the Appellant that while preparing the merit list, GPSC has ignored the judgment of this Court in Jitendra Kumar Singh and Anr. v. State of Uttar Pradesh and Ors.,. Therefore, the Appellant filed Special Civil Application before the learned Single Judge of the High Court challenging correctness of the aforesaid select list. Learned Single Judge allowed the application. Being aggrieved and dissatisfied with the order of the learned Single Judge, GPSC filed Letters Patent. The Division Bench of the High Court by order has allowed the appeal and set aside the order of the learned Single Judge holding that, all those candidates belonging to a reserved category, if they avail the benefit of age relaxation, same was to be considered as relaxation in standard and therefore, such candidates who got benefit of age relaxation were not entitled to be considered in general category and their cases are required to be considered for reserved category cases only. In this appeal, the Appellant has challenged the legality and correctness of the aforesaid order of the Division Bench of the High Court.

Held, while dismissing the appeal:

i. Thus, the appointments in the category of SC/ST and other backward classes to the post of class I and class III in the State Services are being governed by the aforesaid policies and the State Government and/or any Authorities effecting direct appointments are required to give effect to the aforesaid policy decision at the time of recruitment process viz. preparing the select list etc.

ii. It is evident from two circulars that, a candidate who has availed of age relaxation in the selection process as a result of belonging to a reserved category cannot, thereafter, seek to be accommodated in or migrated to the general category seats.

iii. In the advertisement published by the GPSC inviting applications from the eligible candidates, upper age limit relaxation was granted to the candidates belonging to SC/ST and SEBC category. It was also specifically stated in the advertisement that if any candidate belonging to reserved category who applies in the open category, such candidate would not get the benefit of age relaxation. Such age relaxation was granted in pursuance to Rule 8 of Rules of 1967.

iv. Article 16(4) of the Constitution is an enabling provision empowering the State to make any provision or reservation of appointments or posts in favour of any backward class of citizens which in the opinion of the State is not adequately represented in the service under the State. It is purely a matter of discretion of the State Government to formulate a policy for concession, exemption, preference or relaxation either conditionally or unconditionally in favour of the backward classes of citizens. The reservation being the enabling provision, the manner and the extent to which reservation is provided has to be spelled out from the orders issued by the Government from time to time.

v. In the instant case, State Government has framed policy for the grant of reservation in favour of SC/ST and OBC by the Circulars dated 21st January, 2000 and 23rd July, 2004. The State Government has clarified that when a relaxed standard is applied in selecting a candidate for SC/ST, SEBC category in the age limit, experience, qualification, permitting number of chances in the written examination etc., then candidate of such category selected in the said manner, shall have to be considered only against his/her reserved post. Such a candidate would be deemed as unavailable for consideration against unreserved post.

vi. It is evident from the advertisement that, a person who avails of an age relaxation at the initial stage will necessarily avail of the same relaxation even at the final stage. Age relaxation granted to the candidates belonging to SC/ST and SEBC category in the instant case is an incident of reservation under Article 16(4) of the Constitution of India. Appeal dismissed.

᭬᭬᭬

ELEVEN

Tamil Nadu Medical Officers' Association and Ors. Vs. Union of India (UOI) and Ors., 2018

Hon'ble Judges/Coram:

Kurian Joseph, Mohan M. Shantanagoudar and Navin Sinha, JJ.

Equivalent Citation: 2018(2)ESC366(SC), 2018(5)SCALE687, 2018(4)SCT253(SC), MANU/SC/0375/2018

Relevant sections: Regulation 9(4) and (8) of Post Graduate Medical Education Regulations, 2000

Number of pages in original Judgment: 06

Case Note:

Law of Medicine - Validity of Regulation - Method for admissions - Regulation 9(4) and (8) of Post Graduate Medical Education Regulations, 2000 - In present writ petitions, Regulation 9(4) and (8) of Post Graduate Medical Education Regulations, 2000, as framed by Medical Council of India, were under challenge - Whether reservation in respect of 50% of State Quota for in-service candidates was sustainable.

Brief Facts:

The main dispute pertains to the claim made by the State for reservation in favour of the in-service candidates in respect of 50% of the seats granted to the States, since 50% of the seats, in any case are set apart for All-India category. It is the main contention of the Petitioners that while "the coordination and determination of standards in institutions for higher education" is within the exclusive domain of the Union, medical education under Entry 25, List III, though made subject to Entry 66 of List I, being an Entry in the Concurrent List, the State is not denuded of its power to legislate on the manner and method for admissions to Post Graduate Medical Courses.

Held, while placing matters before the Hon'ble CJI for consideration by a larger Bench:

i.   It is submitted that, though Regulation 9(4) provides for 10% incentive for every year of service in remote/difficult/rural areas up to a maximum of 30% of the score, the provision will not ensure to the benefit of the in-service candidates. It is pointed out that, the States have been following, for several reasons and for several years, the pattern of reservation in respect of 50% of State Quota for the in-service candidates. It is submitted that even in that 50%, the list can be prepared by providing the incentive for the service in difficult, rural or remote areas. It is also pointed out that the Regulations also have considered the power of the State to provide for reservation. This can be seen from Regulation 9(8) which provides for reservation of 50% of the seats in Post Graduate Diploma Courses for medical officers in Government service in the State who have served for at least three years in remote and difficult areas with a further condition of minimum continued service of two years in such areas. It is also the contention of the Petitioners that, if there can be such a reservation in the case of Post Graduate Diploma Courses, there is no justification for denying such a reservation in case of the Post Graduate Degree Courses.

ii. On behalf of the Union of India and the Medical Council of India, it is pointed out that once an Entry is provided under List I, it is the exclusive domain of the Union and even if the Union has not legislated exhaustively in respect of that Entry, the State cannot legislate on that subject. Reference has been invited to the decision of this Court in Gujarat University and Anr. v. Krishna Ranganath Mudholkar and Ors.

In any case, it is pointed out that all the contentions raised by the Petitioners have been considered in Dinesh Singh Chauhan and, therefore, the writ petitions are only to be dismissed.

iii. State of Uttar Pradesh and Ors. v. Dinesh Singh Chauhan, has not considered the legislative Entries in respect of the contentions noted above. Apparently, it appears no such contentions were raised before the Court. Same is the situation with regard to the non-reference with respect to the three Constitution Bench decisions we have referred to above. As far as Modern Dental is concerned, perhaps the judgment had not been published by the time the judgment in State of Uttar Pradesh and Ors. v. Dinesh Singh Chauhan was rendered.

iv. The Petitioners have raised several other contentions and invited reference to the judgments by Benches of equal strength as in State of Uttar Pradesh and Ors. v. Dinesh Singh Chauhan.

v. Present writ petitions require consideration by a larger Bench.

vi. Even the interim relief should be considered by the larger Bench.

vii. Accordingly, place the matters before the Hon'ble the Chief Justice of India for consideration by a larger Bench.

ppp

TWELVE

B.K. PAVITRA AND ORS. VS. UNION OF INDIA (UOI) AND ORS., 2017

Hon'ble Judges/Coram:

Adarsh Kumar Goel and U.U. Lalit, JJ.

Equivalent Citation: AIR2017SC820, 2017(2) AKR 155, 2017(1)ESC169(SC), ILR 2017 1361, 2017(2)KarLJ369, 2017LabIC1075, 2017(2)LLN273(SC), 2017(2)SCALE296, (2017)4SCC620, (2017)2SCC(LS)128, 2017 (2) SCJ 379, 2017(2)SCT192(SC), 2017(2)SLJ226(SC), 2017(3)SLR226(SC), MANU/SC/0143/2017

Relevant sections: Articles 14, Article 16 and Article 335 of Constitution of India, 1950; Rule 4 or Rule 4A of the 1957 Rules

Number of pages in original Judgment: 16

Case Note:

Service - Grant of consequential seniority - Validity of Act - Reservation policy - Karnataka Determination of Seniority of Government Servants Promoted on the Basis of Reservation (To the Posts in the Civil Services of the State) Act, 2002 and Articles 14 and 16 of Constitution of India - Present appeals dealt with validity of Act - High Court held Act to be valid - Whether Act is consistent with Articles 14 and 16 of Constitution

Brief Facts:

The present appeals involved the question of validity of the Karnataka Determination of Seniority of the Government Servants Promoted on the Basis of Reservation (To the Posts in the Civil Services of the State) Act, 2002 (the impugned Act). Such Act provides for grant of consequential seniority to the Government servants belonging to Scheduled Castes and the Scheduled Tribes promoted under reservation policy. It also protects consequential seniority already accorded from 27th April, 1978 onwards. The validity of the Act was challenged before the present Court in the case of M. Nagaraj and Ors. v. Union of India and others. The issue referred to larger Bench was decided by this Court. While upholding the constitutional validity of the Constitution (seventy-seventh Amendment) Act, 1995; the Constitution (Eighty-first Amendment) Act, 2000; the Constitution (Eighty-Second Amendment) Act, 2000 and the Constitution (Eighty-fifth Amendment) Act, 2001, individual matters were remitted to the appropriate Bench. Thereafter, the matter was remitted back to the High Court for deciding the question of validity of the said enactment. The High Court by the impugned judgment held the Act to be valid.

A Policy of reservation in promotion was introduced in the State vide Government Order dated 27th April, 1978. The reservation in promotion was provided to the SCs and STs to the extent of 15% and 3% respectively but upto and inclusive of the lowest Group-A posts in the cadres where there is no element of direct recruitment and where the direct recruitment does not exceed $66\frac{2}{3}$ %. A roster of 33 points was issued applicable to each cadre of posts under each appointing authority. Prior to 1st April, 1992, there was no carry forward system of the vacancies. It was introduced on 1st April, 1992. In the stream of graduate Engineers, the reservation in promotion was available upto and inclusive of third level, i.e., Executive Engineers upto 1999 and on the date of fling of the petition (in 2002), it was available upto second level, i.e. Assistant Executive Engineer. In Diploma Engineers, it was available upto third level, i.e. Assistant Executive Engineer-Division II. According to the Appellants, Assistant Engineers of SC/ST category recruited in the year 1987 were promoted to the cadre of Assistant Executive Engineers while in general merit, Assistant Engineers recruited in 1976 were considered for promotion to the said cadre. According to the Appellants, SC/ST candidates got promotion early and on account of consequential seniority, percentage of SC/ST candidates was much higher than the permitted percentage and all top positions were likely to be filled up by SC/ST candidates without general merit candidates getting to higher positions. This aspect was considered in the judgment of this Court in M.G. Badappanavar v. State of Karnataka. This Court issued a direction to the State of Karnataka to redo the seniority and take further action in the light of the said judgments. Pointing out the consequence of accelerated seniority to the roster point promotee, it was averred in the writ petition that the roster point promotee would reach the third level by the age of 45 and fourth, fifth and sixth level in next three, two and two years. The general merit promotee would reach the third level only at the age of 56 and retire before reaching the fourth level. This would result in reverse discrimination and representation of reserved category would range between 36% to 100%. Stand of the State and the contesting Respondents who were given promotion under the reservation, was that inter se seniority amongst persons promoted on any occasion is determined as per Karnataka Government Servants (Seniority) Rules, 1957 (1957 Rules). By amendment dated 1st April, 1992 provision was made to fill-up backlog vacancies which was upheld by this Court in Bhakta Ramegowda v. State of Karnataka. On that basis, Government order dated 24th June, 1997 was issued for fixation of seniority of SC/ST candidates promoted under reservation. Thus, all candidates promoted 'on the same occasion' retained their seniority in the lower cadre. This aspect was not considered in Badappanavar. Extent of reservation for SC and ST was 15% and 3% respectively on the basis of census figures of 1951, though the population of SCs and STs had substantially increased. As per census figures of 1991 population of SC and ST was 16.38% and 4.26% respectively. The stand of the Appellants that the SC/ST candidates reach level four at 45 years or become Chief Engineers by 49 years or there was reverse discrimination had been denied. The matter was put in issue before the High Court. The contention raised on behalf of the Appellants was that grant of consequential seniority to candidates promoted by way of reservation affected efficiency of administration and was violative of Articles 14 and 16. The High Court referring to this Court's judgment in M. Nagaraj observed that concept of "catch up" Rule and "consequential seniority" are judicially evolved concepts to control the effect of reservations. Deleting the said Rule cannot by itself be in conflict with "equality code" under the Constitution. The 85th Amendment gave freedom to the State to provide for reservation in promotion with consequential seniority Under Article 16(4-A) if 'backwardness', 'inadequacy of representation' and 'overall efficiency' so warranted. There was no fixed yardstick to identify and measure the above three factors. If the State fails to identify and measure the above three factors, the reservation can be invalid. Examining whether the State had in fact measured the above factors, the High Court observed that Order dated 27th April, 1978 was issued by the State after considering the statistics available about the representation of SCs and STs in promotional vacancies. On 3rd February, 1999, the policy was modified to limit reservation in promotion in cadre upto and inclusive of the lowest category of Group-A posts in which there is no element of recruitment beyond 66⅔ %. The said order was further amended on 13th April, 1999 to the effect that reservation in the promotion for SCs and STs will continue to operate till their representation reached 15% or 3% respectively and promotion of SCs and STs and against backlog was to continue as per order dated 24th June, 1997 till the said percentage was so reached in the total working strength. As per the Karnataka Scheduled Castes, Scheduled Tribes and other Backward Classes (Reservation of seats in Educational Institutions and of appointments or posts in the services under the State) Act, 1994 (the Karnataka Act 43 of 1994), seniority in the lower cadre is maintained in promotional posts for the persons promoted "on one occasion". Since reservation had not exceeded 15% and 3% for SCs and STs while population of the said categories had increased, there was adequate consideration of the above three factors of "backwardness", inadequacy of representation" and "overall efficiency". Section 3 of the Act provided for an inbuilt mechanism for providing reservation in promotion to the extent of 15% and 3% respectively for the SCs and STs. The State Government collects statistics every year. The High Court held that contention that if all the posts in higher echelons may be filled by SCs and STs, the promotional prospects of general merit candidates will get choked or blocked could not be accepted as reservation in promotion was provided only upto the cadre of Assistant Executive Engineers. It was further observed that there was no pleading that overall efficiency of service would be hampered by promoting persons belonging to SCs and Sts.

Held, while allowing the appeals:

i. The preamble of the impugned Act refers to policy of reservation in promotion in favour of Government servants belonging to SCs and STs in terms of order dated 27th April, 1978. Para 7 of the said order stipulates that inter se seniority amongst persons promoted in accordance with the said order has to be determined in the manner provided under Rule 4 or Rule 4A of the 1957 Rules. There is further reference to the judgment of this Court in Badappanavar (supra) to the effect that there was no specific Rule permitting seniority to be counted for persons promoted against a reserved roster point. It further refers to the Constitution (85th Amendment) Act, 2001 permitting consequential seniority in the case of promotion on the basis of reservation. It states that to remove any ambiguity and to clarify that government servants belonging to SCs and STs promoted in accordance with the reservation in promotion shall be entitled to seniority as it is available to government servants belonging to other categories. Section 3 of the impugned Act provides that government servants belonging to SCs and STs promoted in accordance with the policy reservation in promotion shall be entitled to consequential seniority on the basis of length of service in a cadre. Proviso to the said Section to the effect that inter se seniority of government servants belonging to SCs/STs and those belonging to unreserved category promoted at the same time by a common order shall be on the basis of inter se seniority in the lower cadre. Section 4 provides for protection of consequential seniority already accorded from 27th April, 1978..

ii. While no doubt in M. Nagaraj, 85th Amendment was upheld with the observation that enabling the State to do away with the 'catch up' rule, a judicially evolved concept to control the effect of reservations, was valid but the exercise of power to do away with the said Rule and providing consequential seniority in favour of roster point promotees of reserved category was subject to the limitation of determining the three factors of 'backwardness', 'inadequacy of representation' and 'overall efficiency'. The High Court brushed aside the said mandatory requirement by simply observing that Section 3 provided for an inbuilt mechanism as the extent of mechanism was limited to 15% and 3% respectively for the SCs and STs which dispensed with any requirement of determining inadequacy of representation or backwardness. High Court further dispensed with the requirement of determining overall efficiency by observing that there was no pleading that overall efficiency would be hampered by promoting persons belonging to SCs and STs. This reasoning in the judgment of the High Court, as submitted, was contrary to the mandate of law as recognized in M. Nagaraj and the view similar to the impugned judgment has been repeatedly disapproved in decisions of this Court.

iii. In M. Nagaraj, this Court considered constitutional validity of 77th, 81st, 82nd and 85th Amendments. In doing so, the Court was concerned with the question whether the amendment infringed the basic structure of the Constitution. It was held that equality is part of the basic structure but in the present context, right to equality is not violated by an enabling provision if exercise of power so justifies. It was held that conferment of enabling power on State Under Article 16(4A) did not by itself violate the basic feature of equality. If the affirmative action stipulated Under Article 16(4A) could be balanced with the need for adequate representation for justice to the backwards while upholding equity for the forwards and efficiency for the entire system with the further observation that the content of a right is defined by the Courts and even while the amendment as such could be upheld, validity of an individual enactment was required to be gone into. If the State wished to exercise its discretion Under Article 16(4A), it was to collect quantifiable data showing backwardness of the class and inadequacy of representation of that class in public employment in addition to compliance with Article 335. It was made clear that even if the State has compelling reasons, as stated above, the State will have to see that its reservation provision does not lead to excessiveness so as to breach the ceiling limit of 50% or obliterate the creamy layer or extend the reservation indefinitely.

iv. The exercise for determining 'inadequacy of representation', 'backwardness' and 'overall efficiency', is a must for exercise of power Under Article 16(4A). Mere fact that there is no proportionate representation in promotional posts for the population of SCs and STs is not by itself enough to grant consequential seniority to promotees who are otherwise junior and thereby denying seniority to those who are given promotion later on account of reservation policy. It is for the State to place material on record that there was compelling necessity for exercise of such power and decision of the State was based on material including the study that overall efficiency is not compromised. In the present case, no such exercise had been undertaken. The High Court erroneously observed that it was for the Petitioners to plead and prove that the overall efficiency was adversely affected by giving consequential seniority to junior persons who got promotion on account of reservation. Plea that persons promoted at the same time were allowed to retain their seniority in the lower cadre was untenable and ignored the fact that a senior person may be promoted later and not at same time on account of roster point reservation. Depriving him of his seniority affects his further chances of promotion. Further plea that seniority was not a fundamental right was equally without any merit in the present context. In absence of exercise Under Article 16(4A), it is the 'catch up' Rule which is fully applies. The impugned judgment was set aside and it was declared that the provisions of the impugned Act to the extent of doing away with the 'catch up' Rule and providing for consequential seniority Under Sections 3 and 4 to persons belonging to SCs and STs on promotion against roster points to be ultra vires Articles 14 and 16 of the Constitution. The judgment would not affect those who had already retired and would not affect financial benefits already taken.

ΦΦΦ

THIRTEEN

STATE OF U.P. AND ORS. VS. DINESH SINGH CHAUHAN, 2016

Hon'ble Judges/Coram:

T.S. Thakur, C.J.I., A.M. Khanwilkar and Dr. D.Y. Chandrachud, JJ.

Equivalent Citation: AIR2016SC3841, 2017(1) ALJ 529, 2016 (118) ALR 527, 2016 5 AWC5376SC, 2016(3)ESC476(SC), (2016)6MLJ582, 2016(8)SCALE16, (2016)9SCC749, 2016 (8) SCJ 22, 2016(4)SCT517(SC), 2016(5)SLR492(SC), MANU/SC/0910/2016

Relevant sections: Regulation 9(2) of Post Graduate Medical Education Regulations, 2000 and Article 14 of Constitution of India

Number of pages in original Judgment: 22

Case Note:

Education - Rural service - Reservation - Government order - Regulation - Applicability and interpretation - Regulation 9(2) of Post Graduate Medical Education Regulations, 2000 and Article 14 of Constitution of India - Three sets of matters before present Court - First was appeals arising from judgment of High Court - High Court quashed Government Order reserving 30 percent seats in post-graduate degree courses in medicine and other disciplines for in-service candidates who had relevant years of rural service in notified and difficult areas - Second was appeal arising from decision of High Court - Third was petition praying for declaration that third Proviso to Regulation 9(2) Regulations, 2000, was unconstitutional and violative of Article 14 of Constitution - Further, seeking direction against Authorities to refrain from disturbing selection of Petitioners or to interfere with their Post Graduate studies which they are presently pursuing - Whether High Court exceeded its jurisdiction in setting aside Government Order, when petition filed by the in-service candidates was limited to equate them with in-service candidates who had experience of working in remote or difficult areas - Whether Regulation 9 envisages reservation of seats for in-service Medical Officers generally for admission to Post Graduate Degree Courses - Whether norm specified in Regulation 9 regarding incentive marks can be termed as excessive and unreasonable - Whether arrangement directed in terms of order by present Court should have prospective effect or also apply to admissions for academic year 2015-16

Brief Facts:

There were three sets of matter before the present Court. The first set of appeals were directed against the common judgment of the Division Bench of the High Court disposing the three Writ Petitions preferred by the in-service Medical Officers in the State challenging the Government Orders so far as it imposed a condition of working of three years in rural or difficult areas as ultra-vires and hit by Article 14, 15 and 16 of the Constitution of India. It was also prayed that No Objection Certificate be issued in favour of the Petitioners for admission in MD/MS/Diploma in UPPGMEE-2015 and for quashing of the declaration of result. The High Court was pleased to hold that the State Government has had no authority to frame any Rules or issue any executive order to provide for reservation in the Post Graduate "Degree" Courses, contrary to the statutory Regulations framed under the Medical Council of India Act, 1956 (Central Enactment). The High Court held that Regulation 9 is a complete Code and the admission process must strictly adhere to the norms stipulated therein. It, thus, proceeded to quash the Government Notification-cum-Government Order and directed that admissions to Post Graduate "Degree" Courses be proceeded strictly on merits amongst the candidates who have obtained requisite minimum marks in the common entrance examination in question. It also noted that as per Regulation 9, at best, the in-service candidates who have worked in remote and difficult areas in the State, as notified by the State Government/ Competent Authority from time to time, alone would be eligible for weightage of marks as incentive at the rate of 10% of the marks obtained for each year of service in such areas upto the maximum of 30% marks obtained in National Eligibility-cum-Entrance Test. The second set of appeal was by Medical Officers of State Medical Colleges seeking admission to

Post Graduate Degree Courses. According to them, they were also eligible candidates in terms of Regulation 9 and should have been considered at the time of preparing a fresh merit list. The said Writ Petition was dismissed by the Division Bench on the finding that it was not feasible for the Department to consider the claim of eligible in-service candidates who had not submitted applications/documents before the notified date. In other words, only those in-service candidates who had submitted applications for grant of admission to the Post Graduate Degree Courses within the stipulated time had been considered. This proceeding was, therefore, the fall out of the interim direction issued by present Court. The third set of proceedings was by students aspiring to take admissions to various Post Graduate "Degree" Courses in the State; and who claim to have been affected by the dispensation specified in the interim order passed by present Court. In that, they had been dislodged from the respective Post Graduate Degree Courses in which they were already admitted in the concerned medical colleges and even started pursuing their courses. The sum and substance of the argument was that the challenge before the High Court in the writ petition filed was at the instance of in-service Medical Officers who had not worked or gained experience in remote and difficult areas in the State and wanted to be equated with their counterparts who were or had worked in remote and/ or difficult areas. The High Court, however, quashed the entire resolution providing for 30% reservation to in-service candidates. Further, by way of interim directions present Court directed preparation of fresh merit list; and on following that direction, several meritorious candidates have been dislodged and pushed back in order of merit because of the weightage or incentive marks given to in-service candidates.

Held, while disposing off the appeal:

i. The challenge before the High Court was limited. However, the High Court having held that the State Government could not have issued such order in violation of Regulation 9, quashed the same. The High Court had invited the parties to advance arguments on the validity of the said Government Order before passing the final order. The High Court relied on the decisions of the Supreme Court and opined that it was not permissible, in law, for the State Government to provide reservation for in-service candidates in Post-Graduate "Degree" courses in violation of Regulation 9. Concededly, action taken on the basis of such a void Government Order would be nothing short of a nullity in law. As a result, the High Court proceeded to issue directions to follow the admission process for Post Graduate "Degree" Courses strictly in conformity with Regulation 9. The High Court thus moulded the relief on the basis of the settled legal position. That approach was un-exceptionable, except that it may be necessary to mould the relief further.

ii. After the interim order was passed by present Court on the basis of assurance given by the State, it was not open for the State Government to contend to the contrary. Notably, the State Government had not prayed for relieving itself from the statement as has been recorded in the order. That interim order, therefore, in one sense was invited by the State Government to strictly follow Regulation 9 by giving a weightage of marks to eligible in-service candidates and redraw the merit list.

iii. A priori, it must be held that the relief claimed in the application filed by the State Government is an ingenious way to overcome the unconditional and unequivocal statement made before present Court. The State Government is obliged to adopt a procedure as is stipulated by the Central Act and Regulations framed thereunder and noted in the interim order.

iv. It is well established that Regulation 9 is a self-contained Code regarding the procedure to be followed for admissions to medical courses. It is also well established that the State has no authority to enact any law much less by executive instructions that may undermine the procedure for admission to Post Graduate Medical Courses enunciated by the Central Legislation and Regulations framed thereunder, being a subject falling within the Entry 66 of List I to the Seventh Schedule of the Constitution.

v. Regulation 9 is a composite provision prescribing procedure for selection of candidates-both for Post Graduate "Degree" as well as Post Graduate "Diploma" Courses. Clause (I) of Regulation 9 mandates that there shall be a single National Eligibility-cum-Entrance Test (hereinafter referred to as NEET) to be conducted by the designated Authority. Clause (II) provides for three per cent seats of the annual sanctioned intake capacity to be earmarked for candidates with locomotory disability of lower limbs. Clause (III) provides for eligibility for admission to any Post Graduate Course in a particular academic year. Clause (IV) is the relevant provision. It provides for reservation of seats in medical colleges/institutions for reserved categories as per applicable laws prevailing in States/Union Territories. From the plain language of the proviso, it is amply clear that it does not envisage reservation for in-service candidates in respect of Post Graduate "Degree" Courses. This proviso postulates giving weightage of marks to "specified in-service candidates" who have worked in notified remote and/or difficult areas in the State - both for Post Graduate "Degree" Courses as also for Post Graduate "Diploma" Courses. Further, the weightage of marks so allotted is required to be reckoned while preparing the merit list of candidates.

vi. In the first place, the decisions pressed into service have considered the provisions regarding admission process governed by the Regulations in force at the relevant time. The admission process in the present case is governed by the Regulations which have come into force from Academic Year 2013-14. This Regulation is a self-contained Code. There is nothing in this Regulation to even remotely indicate that a separate channel for admission to in-service candidates must be provided, at least in respect of Post Graduate "Degree" Courses. In contradistinction, however, 50% seats are earmarked for the Post Graduate "Diploma" Courses for in-service candidates, as is discernible from Clause (VII). If the Regulation intended a similar separate channel for in-service candidates even in respect of Post Graduate "Degree" Courses, that position would have been made clear in Regulation 9 itself. In absence thereof, it must be presumed that a separate channel for in-service candidates is not permissible for admission to Post Graduate "Degree" Courses. Thus, the State Government, in law, had no authority to issue a Government Order such as dated 28th February 2014, to provide to the contrary. Hence, the High Court was fully justified in setting aside the said Government Order being contrary to the mandate of Regulation 9 of the Regulations of 2000, as applicable from Academic Year 2013-14.

vii. The real effect of Regulation 9 is to assign specified marks commensurate with the length of service rendered by the candidate in notified remote and difficult areas in the State linked to the marks obtained in NEET. That is a procedure prescribed in the Regulation for determining merit of the candidates for admission to the Post Graduate "Degree" Courses for a single State. This serves a dual purpose. Firstly, the fresh qualified Doctors will be attracted to opt for rural service, as later they would stand a good chance to get admission to Post Graduate "Degree" Courses of their choice. Secondly, the Rural Health Care Units run by the Public Authority would be benefited by Doctors willing to work in notified rural or difficult areas in the State. A Regulation such as this subserves larger public interest.

viii. Regulation 9 does not permit preparation of two merit lists. Regulation 9 is a complete Code. It prescribes the basis for determining the eligibilities of the candidates including the method to be adopted for determining the inter se merit, on the basis of one merit list of candidates appearing in the same NEET including by giving commensurate weightage of marks to the in-service candidates.

ix. Regulations have been framed by an Expert Body based on past experience and including the necessity to reckon the services and experience gained by the in-service candidates in notified remote and difficult areas in the State. The proviso prescribes the measure for giving incentive marks to in-service candidates who have worked in notified remote and difficult areas in the State. That can be termed as a qualitative factor for determining their merit. Even the quantitative factor to reckon merit of the eligible in-service candidates is spelt out in the proviso. It envisages giving of incentive marks at the rate of 10% of the marks obtained for each year of service in remote and/or difficult areas up to 30% of the marks obtained in NEET. It is an objective method of linking the incentive marks to the marks obtained in NEET by the candidate. To illustrate, if an in-service candidate who has worked in a notified remote and/or difficult area in the State for at least one year and has obtained 150 marks out of 200 marks in NEET, he or she would get 15 additional marks; and if the candidate has worked for two years, the candidate would get another 15 marks. Similarly if the candidate has worked for three years and more, the candidate would get a further 15 marks in addition to the marks secured in NEET. 15 marks out of 200 marks in that sense would work out to a weightage of 7.5% only, for having served in notified remote and/or difficult areas in the State for one year. Had it been a case of giving 10% marks enbloc of the total marks irrespective of the marks obtained by the eligible in-service candidates in NEET, it would have been a different matter. Accordingly, some weightage marks given to eligible in-service candidate linked to performance in NEET and also the length of service in remote and/or difficult areas in the State by no standard can be said to be excessive, unreasonable or irrational. This provision has been brought into force in larger public interest and not merely to provide institutional preference or for that matter to create separate channel for the in-service candidate, much less reservation. It is unfathomable as to how such a provision can be said to be unreasonable or irrational.

x. The procedure evolved in Regulation 9 in general and the proviso to Clause (IV) in particular is just, proper and reasonable and also fulfill the test of Article 14 of the Constitution, being in larger public interest.

xi. Ordinarily, as the subject matter of challenge before the High Court was pertaining to Academic Year 2015-16, the dispensation directed in terms of Order dated 12th May 2016 should apply thereto. However, considering the fact that the said admission process has been completed and all concerned have acted upon on that basis and that the candidates admitted to the respective Post Graduate Degree Courses in the concerned colleges have also commenced their studies, it may not be appropriate to unsettle that position given the fact that neither the direct candidates nor the eligible in-service candidates who had worked in remote and/or difficult areas in the State approached the Court for such relief. It is only the in-service candidates who had not worked in remote and/or difficult areas in the State approached the Court for equating them with their counterparts who had worked in remote and/or difficult areas in the matter of reservation of seats for in-service candidates. If at this distance of time, the settled admissions were to be disturbed by quashing the entire admission process for Academic Year 2015-16, it would inevitably result in all the seats in the State almost over 500 in number remaining unfilled for one academic year; and that the candidates to be admitted on the basis of fresh list for Academic Year 2015-16 will have to take fresh admission coinciding with the admissions for Academic Year 2016-17. That would necessitate doubling the strength of seats in the respective colleges for the current Academic Year to accommodate all those students, which may not be feasible and is avoidable. In the peculiar facts on hand, the relief was moulded in the appeals before by directing all concerned to follow the admission process for Academic Year 2016-17 and onwards strictly in conformity with the Regulations in force, governing the procedure for selection of candidates for Post Graduate Medical Degree Courses and including determination of relative merit of the candidates who had appeared in NEET by giving weightage of incentive marks to eligible in-service candidates.

xii. The High Court was justified in quashing the stated Government Order providing for reservation to in-service candidates, being violative of Regulation 9 as in force. However, while modifying the operative direction given by the High Court, direction was made that admission process for Academic Year 2016-17 onwards to the Post Graduate Degree

Course in the State should proceed as per Regulation 9 including by giving incentive marks to eligible in-service candidates in terms of proviso to Clause IV of Regulation 9.

xiii. Regarding the second set of appeals, the view taken by the High Court that the direction to prepare fresh merit list vide interim order was in respect of only such eligible in-service candidates as had submitted applications for admission to Post Graduate Degree Courses for the relevant academic year within stipulated time. The direction in the interim order was not to consider all similarly placed persons (eligible in-service candidates) irrespective of whether they had made applications for admission to Post Graduate Degree Courses or otherwise. Hence, this appeal must fail.

xiv. Even third petition should fail as Regulation 9 to be a complete Code and a provision for determining inter-se merit of the candidates including by giving weightage of marks as incentive to eligible in-service candidates who have worked in notified remote or difficult areas in the State, which is just, reasonable and necessary in larger public interest.

 PPP

FOURTEEN

S. Panneer Selvam and Ors. vs. Government of Tamil Nadu and Ors., 2015

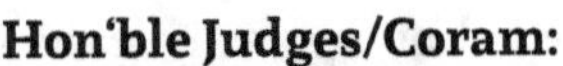

Hon'ble Judges/Coram:

T.S. Thakur and R. Banumathi, JJ.

Equivalent Citation: 2015XI AD (S.C.) 169, 2015 (5) AWC 5020 (SC), 2016(4)CTC189, 2015(4)J.L.J.R.144, 2015(3)JKJ1[SC], 2016(3)LLN550(SC), 2016-2-LW685, 2015(4)PLJR298, 2015(9)SCALE350, (2015)10SCC292, (2016)1SCC(LS)76, 2015 (10) SCJ 750, 2015(4)SCT299(SC), MANU/SC/0937/2015

Relevant sections: Article 16(4A) of Constitution of India; Rule 12, Tamil Nadu Highways Engineering Service Rules

Number of pages in original Judgment: 13

Case Note:

Constitution - Promotion based on reservation - Section 16(4A) Constitution of India, 1950 and Rule 12, Tamil Nadu Highways Engineering Service Rules - State allowed to give consequential seniority to appointments under reserved category under Article 16(4A) - No provision by State in Rules expressly including consequential seniority - Reserved category Respondents promoted ahead of more senior general category

Appellants - Whether in the absence of policy decision by State under Article 16(4A) Constitution the Respondents can be promoted on the basis of reservation before the Appellants.

Service - Consequential seniority - Respondents appointed and promoted on the basis of reservation - Senior Appellants in general category overlooked - Catch-up rule not applied for Appellants - Respondents given benefit of consequential seniority - No specific provision for accelerated promotion of Respondents in Rules - Single judge of High Court set aside seniority list in favour of Appellant - Division Bench on appeal set aside earlier order - Whether the Division Bench erred in disallowing application of the 'catch-up rule' - Whether the Division Bench was right in holding that Article 16(4A) Constitution gives consequential seniority in addition to accelerated promotion to the Respondents.

Brief Facts:

The Appellants were graduate Assistant Engineers and Respondents were Diploma holder Junior Engineers. The categories of Assistant Engineers and Junior Engineers were feeder categories to the category of Assistant Divisional Engineer(ADE) and the first three vacancies to be filled by Assistant Engineers and the fourth vacancy to be filled by recruitment by transfer by Junior Engineer. Rule 12 of Rules prescribes application of rule of reservation for the appointment of ADEs by direct recruitment and recruitment by transfer.

On 29.04.2004, seniority list of ADEs was published by applying 'catch-up rule' among ADEs appointed from Assistant Engineers and consequential seniority was not given to SC/ST ADEs appointed from Assistant Engineers. But the 'catch-up rule' was not applied among the ADEs appointed from Junior Engineers, giving benefit of consequential seniority to SC/ST ADEs appointed from Junior Engineers in addition to accelerated promotion. The Appellants, against the seniority list dated 29.04.2004 and the subsequent seniority list for further promotion to the post of Divisional Engineer dated 19.08.2005, petitioned the High Court. It was contended that the promotion given to Junior Engineers as ADEs was based on rule of reservation and in the promotional post it would not reverse the seniority of the seniors in the feeder category who gained promotions subsequently. The Single Judge of the High Court allowed the petitions by setting aside the seniority list dated 29.04.2004. On appeal by the Respondents, the Division Bench set aside the order of the Single Judge holding that the object of Article 16(4A) of the Constitution was to give accelerated promotion to roster-point promotees in addition to accelerated promotion and the 'catch-up rule' was not applicable. Hence, the present appeals.

Held, allowing the appeals:

i. Article 16(4A) of the Constitution is only an enabling provision which provides that the State may make any provision for providing reservation of appointments or posts in favour of any backward class citizens not adequately represented in the services under the State. In the absence of any policy decision taken by the State, Article 16(4A) of the Constitution will not protect the consequential seniority granted to the Respondents who were promoted to the post of Assistant Divisional Engineers following the rule of reservation. Rule 12 of the Rules does not provide for the consequential seniority for reserved category promotees. In the absence of any specific provision or policy decision taken by the State Government for consequential seniority for reserved category accelerated promotees, there is no automatic application of Article 16(4A) of the Constitution.

ii. Determination of seniority is a vital aspect in the service career of an employee and his future promotion is dependent on this. Thus, determination of seniority must be based on principles which are just and fair. In the absence of any policy decision taken or rules framed by the State regarding the services, accelerated promotion given to the Respondents following the rule of reservation in terms of Rule 12 of the Rules will not give them consequential accelerated seniority. The claim of inadequacy of representation of SC/STs in the services by itself is not sufficient to uphold such an inadequacy. Even under Article 16(4) of the Constitution, the State is duty bound to collect data to assess the adequacy of representation of SC/ST candidates in the service. No material is adduced that such an exercise was undertaken to collect data of adequacy of representation of the SC/ST candidates in the services. In the absence of any rule conferring consequential seniority in the State 'catch up rule' is applicable even amongst Junior Engineers promoted as ADEs following rule of reservation and also for their seniority amongst Assistant Engineerss promoted as ADEs and Junior Engineers promoted as ADEs.

iii. There is no merit in the Respondents' contention that since they were initially appointed as Junior Engineers and the Appellants as Assistant

Engineers, there is no common seniority between the two. Both the Assistant Engineers and the Junior Engineers are feeder categories for filling up higher post of the Assistant Divisional Engineer in the ratio of 3:1, respectively. Moreover, prior to 1993 both categories used to be classified as one category of service. It was only by Government Order dated 24.05.1993, the post of Assistant Engineer was raised to the present level. For promotion, even though two separate seniority lists are prepared for each category, they are actually of the same cadre.In the absence of any provision for consequential seniority in the rules, the 'catch up rule' will be applicable and the Respondents cannot count their seniority in the promoted category from the date of their promotion and the senior general candidates if later reach the promotional level, general candidates will regain their seniority. The judgment of the Division Bench is set aside.

ᐒᐒᐒ

FIFTEEN

CHAIRMAN AND MANAGING DIRECTOR CENTRAL BANK OF INDIA VS. CENTRAL BANK OF INDIA SC/ST EMPLOYEES WELFARE ASSOCIATION, 2015

Hon'ble Judges/Coram:

Jasti Chelameswar and A.K. Sikri, JJ.

Equivalent Citation: 2015(2)ABR302, 2015I AD (S.C.) 313, 2015(2)AJR245, 2015 (2) AWC 1354 (SC), 120(2015)CLT668(SC), 2015(1)ESC134(SC), 2015(1)J.L.J.R.421, 2015LabIC981, 2015(2)PLJR13, 2015(1)SCALE169, (2015)12SCC308, (2016)1SCC(LS)355, 2015 (2) SCJ 312, 2015(2)SCT54(SC), 2015(1)SLJ372(SC), 2015(2)SLR17(SC), (2015)1UPLBEC369, MANU/SC/0017/2015

Relevant sections: Article 16(4) of Constitution of India

Number of pages in original Judgment: 13

Case Note:

Constitution - Promotion - Reservation - Office Memorandum - High Court made direction that selection of in-service medical officers for post-graduate medical education should be made strictly on basis of inter se seniority of candidates who had taken common entrance test - Hence, present appeal - Whether selection of in-service medical officers for post-graduate medical education should be made strictly on basis of inter se seniority of candidates - Held, Office Memorandum reflect that in promotion by selection within Class-I (Group-A)post, SC/ST candidates were to be given 'concession' - Said concession was available to those SC/ST employees who were senior enough in zone of consideration for promotion so as to be within number of vacancies for which select list had to be drawn up - Said Memorandum did not make any new provision for reservation in promotion in favour of SC/ST employees - Impugned judgment of High Court set aside to extent it holds that Office Memorandum makes provision for reservation - Clarified that at present there was no provision for reservation in promotion by selection only in respect of those posts which carry ultimate salary - It would have effect of allowing writ petitions filed by Respondents/unions partly with directions to Appellant Banks to make provision for reservations while carrying out promotions from Scale-I to Scale-II and upward upto Scale- VI - Appeal disposed of.

Brief facts:

The issue which arises for consideration in these appeals lies within a narrow campus and is crisp one, though at the same time it is of seminal importance for the parties before us. It relates to the rule of reservation of the Scheduled Castes (SC) and Scheduled Tribes (ST) in the promotion in the officer grade/scale in the Appellant Banks. There is no dispute that the Appellant Banks, which are statutory/public sector banks, are following the applicable guidelines of the Central Government pertaining to reservation of SC and ST employees insofar as their promotion from clerical grade to officer grade is concerned. The question to be answered is as to whether there is any reservation in the promotions from one officer grade/scale to another grade/scale, when such promotions are made on selection basis. As per the Appellant Banks, there is no rule of reservation for promotion in the Class A (Class-I) to the posts/scales having basic salary of more than ' 5,700/- and in the relevant instructions, issued in the form of Office Memoranda, only a concession is provided in the manner officers belonging to SC/ST category are to be considered for promotion. To put it otherwise, the position taken by the Banks is that there is no rule of reservation for promotions and the candidature of these officers belonging to these categories for promotion is to be considered on the basis of relaxed standards. The Respondents, who are SC/ST Employees' Unions of the Appellant Banks or individuals belonging to such categories, dispute the aforesaid stand taken by the Banks. According to them, the circular issued by the Central Government expressly provides for such a reservation.

It is interesting to note that for taking their respective positions both the parties rely upon O.M. dated 13-08-1997 issued by the Central Government (which, of course, is to be read along with other connected office memoranda). Thus, outcome of these appeals would depend upon the interpretation that is to be accorded to the said Office Memorandum dated 13-08-1997. As the Banks are in appeal against the judgment of High Court of Judicature at Madras rendered on 09-12-2009 whereby number of writ appeals were disposed of, it can clearly be discerned that insofar as High Court is concerned its interpretation to the aforesaid circular has gone in favour of the SC/ST employees.

Held, while disposing off the appeal:

Upshot of the aforesaid discussion would be to allow these appeals partly. While setting aside the impugned judgment of the High Court to the extent it holds that Office Memorandum dated 13-08-1997 makes a provision for reservation, it is clarified that at present there is no provision for reservation in promotion by selection only in respect of those posts which carry an ultimate salary of ' 5,700/- per month (revised to ' 18,300/- by 5th Central Pay Commission and ' 20,800/- per month in respect of those Public Sector Undertakings following IDA pattern). *Qua* Appellant Banks, that would be in respect of Scale-VII and above. Therefore, to carry out promotions from Scale-I upwards upto Scale-VI, reservation in promotion in favour of SC/ST employees has to be given. It would have the effect of allowing the writ petitions filed by the Respondents/unions partly with directions to the Appellant Banks to make provision for reservations while carrying out promotions from Scale-I to Scale-II and upward upto Scale-VI. In view of the above, Contempt Petition (Civil) No. 320 of 2010 is disposed off with directions to the Appellant Banks to carry out the promotions by adopting the procedure mentioned in this judgment. In the peculiar facts of this case, we leave the parties to bear their own costs.

ppp

SIXTEEN

U.P. POWER CORPORATION LTD. AND ORS. VS. RAJESH KUMAR AND ORS., 2012

Hon'ble Judges/Coram:

Dalveer Bhandari and Dipak Misra, JJ.

Equivalent Citation: 2012(5)ADJ19, 2012(5)ADJ19, AIR2012SC2728, 2012 4 AWC4136SC, [2012(134)FLR692], 2012(2)J.L.J.R.454, 2012(4)KarLJ87, 2012LabIC2267, 2012(3)PLJR55, 2012(4)SCALE687, (2012)7SCC1, 2012(2)SLJ307(SC), 2012(4)SLR1(SC), MANU/SC/0334/2012

Relevant sections: Articles 16(4A), 16(4B) and 335 of Constitution of India, 1950; Section 3(7) of Reservation Act, 1994; Rule 8A of Uttar Pradesh Government Servant Seniority (3rd amendment) Rules, 2007

Number of pages in original Judgment: 23

Case Note:

Constitution - Validity of provision - Articles 16(4A), 16(4B) and 335 of Constitution of India, 1950; Section 3(7) of Reservation Act, 1994; Rule 8A of Uttar Pradesh Government Servant Seniority (3rd amendment) Rules, 2007 - Controversy pertaining to reservation in promotion for Scheduled Castes and Scheduled Tribes with consequential seniority as engrafted under Articles 16(4A) and 16(4B) of Constitution and facet of relaxation grafted by way of a proviso to Article 335 of Constitution of India, being incorporated by Constitution (Seventy-seventh Amendment) Act, 1995, the Constitution

(Eight-first Amendment) Act, 2000, Constitution (Eighty-second Amendment) Act, 2000 and Constitution (Eighty-fifth Amendment) Act, 2001 at various stages having withstood judicial scrutiny by dictum in M. Nagaraj v. Union of India - Whether Section 3(7) of 1994 Act and Rule 8A of 2007 Rules were ultra vires and liable to be held invalid - Held, vesting of power by an enabling provision might be constitutionally valid and yet 'exercise of power' by State in a given case might be arbitrary, particularly, if State failed to identify and measure backwardness and inadequacy keeping in mind efficiency of service as required under Article 335 of Constitution - Article 16(4) of Constitution, which protected interests of certain sections of society had to be balanced against Article 16(1) of Constitution, which protected interests of every citizen of entire society - They should be harmonized because, they were restatements of principle of equality under Article 14 of Constitution - Each post get marked for particular category of candidates to be appointed against it and any subsequent vacancy had to be filled by that category candidate - Appropriate Government had to apply cadre strength as a unit in operation of roster in order to ascertain whether a given class/group was adequately represented in service - Cadre strength as a unit also ensured that, upper ceiling-limit of 50% was not violated - Further roster had to be post-specific and not vacancy based - State had to form its opinion on quantifiable data regarding adequacy of representation - Clause (4A) of Article 16 of Constitution, was an enabling provision. It gave freedom to State to provide for reservation in matters of promotion - Clause (4A) of Article 16 of Constitution, applied only to SCs and STs - Said clause was carved out of Article 16(4A) of Constitution - Therefore, Clause (4A) would be governed by two compelling reasons - "backwardness" and "inadequacy of representation", as mentioned in Article 16(4) of Constitution - If said two reasons did not exist, then enabling provision could not be enforced - If ceiling-limit on carry-over of unfilled vacancies was removed, other alternative time-factor came in and in that event, time-scale had to be imposed in interest of efficiency in administration as mandated by Article 335 of Constitution - If time-scale was not kept, then posts would continue to remain vacant for years which would be detrimental to administration - Therefore, in each case, appropriate Government would now have to introduce duration depending upon fact-situation - If appropriate Government enacted a law providing for reservation without keeping in mind parameters in Article 16(4) of Constitution and Article 335 of Constitution, then this Court would certainly set aside and strike down such legislation - Constitutional limitation under Article 335 of Constitution, was relaxed and not obliterated - Concepts of efficiency, backwardness and inadequacy of representation were required to be identified and measured - That exercise depended on availability of data - That exercise depended on numerous factors - It was for this reason that, enabling provisions were required to be made because each competing claim sought to achieve certain goals - How best one should optimize these conflicting claims could only be done by administration in context of local prevailing conditions in public employment - Article 16(4) of Constitution, therefore, created a field which enabled a State to provide for reservation provided there exists backwardness of a class and inadequacy of representation in employment - These were compelling reasons - They did not exist in Article 16(1) of Constitution - It was only, when these reasons were satisfied that a State get the power to provide for reservation in matter of employment - Articles 16(4A) and 16(4B) of Constitution, were enabling provisions and State could make provisions for same on certain basis or foundation - Conditions precedent had not been satisfied - No exercise had been undertaken - When provisions of Constitution were treated valid with certain conditions or riders, it became incumbent on part of State to appreciate and apply test so that, its amendments could be tested and withstand scrutiny on parameters laid down therein - Section 3(7) of 1994 Act and Rule 8A of 2007 Rules were ultra vires, as they ran counter to dictum in M. Nagaraj - Any promotion that had been given on dictum of Indra Sawhney and without aid or assistance of Section 3(7) and Rule 8A should remain undisturbed - Appeals arising out of final judgment of Division Bench at Allahabad were allowed and impugned order was set aside - Appeals arising out of judgment from Division Bench at Lucknow was affirmed subject to modification.

Brief Facts:

i. Extraordinary and, in a way, perplexing though it may seem, yet as the factual scenario pronouncedly reveals, the assail in some of the appeals of this batch of appeals is to the judgment and order passed by the Division Bench of the High Court of Judicature at Allahabad in Writ Petition No. 63217 of 2010 (Mukund Kumar Srivastava v. State of U.P. and Anr. upholding the validity of the provisions contained in Rule 8-A of the U.P. Government Servants Seniority Rules, 1991 (for brevity 'the 1991 Rules') that were inserted by the U.P. Government Servants Seniority (3rd Amendment) Rules, 2007 by the employees-Appellants and in some of the appeals, the challenge by the State Government and the U.P. Power Corporation Ltd. (for short 'the Corporation') is to the judgment and order passed by the Division Bench of the High Court of Judicature at Allahabad, Lucknow Bench, Lucknow, in Writ Petition No. 1389 (S/B) of 2007 (Prem Kumar Singh and Ors. v. State of U.P. and Ors. and other connected writ petitions holding, inter alia, that the decision rendered by the Division Bench in the case of Mukund Kumar Srivastava (supra) at Allahabad is per incuriam and not a binding precedent and further Section 3(7) of the Uttar Pradesh Public Servants (Reservation for Scheduled Castes, Scheduled Tribes and other Backward Classes) Act, 1994 (for short 'the 1994 Act') and Rule 8A of the 1991 Rules, as brought into force in 2007, are invalid, ultra vires and unconstitutional and, as a necessary corollary, the consequential orders relating to seniority passed by the State Government deserved to be quashed and, accordingly, quashed the same and further clarified that in case the State Government decides to provide reservation in promotion to any class or classes of posts in the services under the State, it is free to do so after undertaking the exercise as required under the constitutional provisions keeping in mind the law laid down by this Court in M. Nagraj (supra). It has been directed that till it is done, no reservation in promotion on any post or classes of posts under the services of the State including the Corporation shall be made hence forth. However, the Division Bench observed that the promotions already made as per the provisions/Rules where the benefit of Rule 8A has not been given while making the promotion shall not be disturbed.

ii. The cleavage has invited immense criticism by the learned senior Counsel appearing for both sides on principles of judicial discipline, decorum, propriety and tradition. Initially the debate centred around the concept of precedent and the duties of the Benches but gradually it was acceded to, absolutely totally being seemly, to decide the controversy on merits instead of a remit and, accordingly, the Learned Counsel for the parties addressed the Court at length. As advised, we shall dwell upon the merits of the controversy but we shall not abdicate our responsibility to delve into the first issue, i.e., judicial discipline as we are inclined to think that it is the duty, nay, obligation in the present case to do so because despite repeated concern shown by this Court, the malady subsists, making an abode of almost permanency. Ergo, we proceed to state the facts on the first issue and our opinion thereon and, thereafter, shall deal with the assail and attack on both the judgments on merits.

Held, while disposing off the appeals:

In the ultimate analysis, we conclude and hold that Section 3(7) of the 1994 Act and Rule 8A of the 2007 Rules are ultra vires as they run counter to the dictum in M. Nagaraj (supra). Any promotion that has been given on the dictum of Indra Sawhney (supra) and without the aid or assistance of Section 3(7) and Rule 8A shall remain undisturbed.

The appeals arising out of the final judgment of Division Bench at Allahabad are allowed and the impugned order is set aside. The appeals arising out of the judgment from the Division Bench at Lucknow is affirmed subject to the modification as stated hereinabove. In view of the aforesaid, all other appeals are disposed of. The parties shall bear their respective costs.

ppp

SEVENTEEN

ANIL CHANDRA AND ORS. VS. RADHA KRISHNA GAUR AND ORS., 2009

Hon'ble Judges/Coram:

Tarun Chatterjee and V.S. Sirpurkar, JJ.

Equivalent Citation: 2010(1)ALLMR(SC)417, 2010(6)ALT5(SC), 2010 (3) AWC 2342 (SC), JT2009(12)SC468, 2009LabIC3923, 2009(12)SCALE417, (2009)9SCC454, (2009)2SCC(LS)683, [2009]14SCR335, 2009(4)SCT560(SC), 2010(1)SLJ224(SC), 2009(7)SLR612(SC), 2009(7)SLR612(SC), 2009(10)UJ4566, MANU/SC/1639/2009

Relevant sections: Article 16(4A) of Constitution of India; Rule 8A of U. P. Government Servants Seniority (3rd Amendment) Rules, 2007

Number of pages in original Judgment: 05

Case Note:

Constitution of India - Article 16 (4A)--U. P. Government Servants Seniority (3rd Amendment) Rules, 2007--Rule 8A--Employment--Promotion--Reservation--Seniority--Amendment Rules pertaining to reservation and promotion list--Are prospective in nature--And thereby cannot disturb promotion list of appellants by virtue of rule--High Court fully justified in granting interim order--No infirmity therein.

Brief Facts:

i. In the year 1973, the Government Orders providing reservation in the matter of promotion for the Scheduled Castes and Scheduled Tribes were issued. Subsequently, the U.P. Jal Nigam adopted the U.P. Government Servants Seniority Rules 1991. The aforesaid rules were notified by the State Government vide Notification dated 20th of March, 1991 which consisted of provisions of the aforesaid Rules of 1991. The respondent No. 2, namely, U.P. Jal Nigam is a Statutory Corporation created under the U.P. Water Supply and Sewerage Act, 1975 and the service conditions of the employees of the Nigam are governed by the U.P. Jal Nigam (Public Health Branch) Service Regulations, 1978. The aforesaid regulations were made in exercise of power conferred on the U.P. Jal Nigam under Sections 97(2) and 98(1) of the U.P. Water Supply and Sewerage Act, 1975 with the prior approval of the State Government.

ii. Subsequently, in the year 1994, the Uttar Pradesh Public Services (Reservation for Schedule Caste, Schedule Tribes and other Backward Classes) Act, 1994 was promulgated and Section 3(7) of the said Act of 1994 says that if on the date of the commencement of this Act, reservation was in force under Government orders for appointment to posts to be filled up by promotion, such Government orders shall continue to be applicable till they are modified or revoked. Further, on 10th of October, 1994 the percentage of reservation in the matter of Schedule Castes was enhanced from 18% to 21% by means of Government order referring to Section 3(7) of the aforesaid Act of 1994.

iii. Article 16(4A) was introduced by an amendment of the Constitution on 17th of June, 1995, which reads as under:

Nothing in this article shall prevent the State from making any provision for reservation in the matters of promotion, with consequential seniority, to any class or class of posts in the services under the State in favour of the scheduled castes and the scheduled tribes which in the opinion of the State are not adequately represented in the services under the State.

i. Article 16(4A) of the Constitution, which was inserted in the Constitution on 17th of June, 1995, as noted herein earlier, was incorporated by the Constitution (77th Amendment) Act, 1995 thereby introducing an enabling provision for providing reservation in the matter of promotion.

Held, while disposing off the petition:

i. Since the interim order passed by the High Court, which has not been interfered with by us in this judgment, we make it clear that the grant of interim order and any observation made by the High Court while granting interim order and any observations made by us in this order shall not influence the High Court to decide the writ petition on merits and the High Court shall not be influenced by any of the observations made by us in this order.

ii. There is one another aspect of this matter. These appeals have been filed, as noted herein earlier, against an interim order passed by the High Court. It appears that the main writ petition, with which the present writ application has been tagged by the High Court, has already been taken up for hearing, which is already heard in part. Such being the position at this stage, it would not be appropriate for us to interfere with the impugned order passed by the High Court at this stage when the writ petition itself can be decided within a very short time.

iii. Considering the importance of the present dispute between the parties, we are of the view that the High Court shall take efforts to decide the writ petitions at an early date and dispose of the same within six months from the date of supply of a copy of this order to it.

ppp

EIGHTEEN

SHIV PRASAD VS. GOVERNMENT OF INDIA AND ORS., 2008

Hon'ble Judges/Coram:

C.K. Thakker and Devinder Kumar Jain, JJ.

Equivalent Citation: 2009(4)ALT27(SC), 2008(3)ESC537(SC), 2008GLH(2)692, JT2008(5)SC422, 2008LabIC3622, 2008(6)SCALE315, (2008)10SCC382, (2009)1SCC(LS)40, 2008(4)SCT522(SC), 2009(2)SLR352(SC), 2009(2)SLR352(SC), (2008)2UPLBEC1684, MANU/SC/7515/2008

Relevant sections: Articles 14, 16, 19 and 21 of the Constitution of India

Number of pages in original Judgment: 08

Ratio Decidendi:

Reservation for women candidates cannot be held invalid or in excess of permissible quota as the reservation policy itself makes clear that reservation will be of Horizontal nature i.e. if any woman candidate is selected on the basis of reservation on any category then she will be fixed of the said category.

Case Note:

Service - Reservation in matter of appointment - Appointment of women in excess of permissible quota - Petitioner challenged appointment of Respondent No. 4 , a woman candidate, to the post of Assistant Professor with Respondent University on ground that same would be in excess of permissible quota - Hence, present writ petition - Held, the reservation for women candidates cannot be held invalid or in excess of permissible quota as the reservation policy itself makes clear that reservation will be of

Horizontal nature i.e. if any woman candidate is selected on the basis of reservation on any category then she will be fixed of the said category - Petition dismissed.

Brief Facts:

Shortly stated the facts of the case are that on August 10, 2000, Roorkee University issued an advertisement for filling up various vacancies in different faculties. The controversy in present appeals relates to the vacancy position in the Department of Mathematics. As observed in the impugned judgment of the High Court, there were six posts of Professors (unreserved) and three posts of Associate/Assistant Professors. Out of three posts, two were reserved for Scheduled Caste candidates while one was for General Category: Unreserved (UR). They were to be filled under Flexible Cadre Structure (FCS) in accordance with reserve roaster notified by the Government of Uttar Pradesh under whose control the University was functioning at the relevant time. Appellants in both the appeals applied in March, 2001. Interviews were conducted on March 20, 2001. Selection Committee met on the next day, i.e. March 21, 2001. It is the case of the writ petitioner that he was selected for the post of Associate Professor. According to him, respondent No. 4 (Dr. Madhu Jain) was not found eligible and was neither selected nor recommended. The writ petitioner, however, did not receive an appointment letter for quite some time. On the contrary, he came to know that respondent No. 4 was intimated by the University that she was selected and being appointed as Assistant Professor in the Department of Mathematics. The writ petitioner made representations. Since there was no favourable reply, he was constrained to approach the High Court by filing a writ petition. The Division Bench of the High Court by the order impugned in the present appeals, allowed his petition, set aside the appointment of respondent No. 4 but directed the University to re-advertise the post and to conduct the selection process afresh. Consequence of the order passed by the High Court was that the writ petitioner succeeded and selection and appointment of respondent No. 4 to the post of Assistant Professor in Mathematics had been set aside, but no effective relief had been granted in favour of writ petitioner. The grievance of the writ petitioner in the present appeal is that though he was eligible, qualified, found fit and recommended for appointment to the post of Associate Professor, he was not appointed. The High Court, no doubt, allowed his writ petition but it was wrong in directing re- advertisement of the post and to conduct selection process afresh. The complaint of respondent No. 4-appellant in the cognate appeal, on the other hand, is that on the facts and in the circumstances of the case, she was rightly selected, recommended and appointed as Assistant Professor in Mathematics and the High Court was not justified in setting aside her appointment. The action of the University in appointing her was legal and valid and ought not to have been disturbed by the High Court.

Held, while dismissing the petition:

For the foregoing reasons, in our view, the appeal filed by Dr. Shiv Prasad (Petitioner of Writ Petition No. 802 (S/B) of 2001) deserves to be dismissed and is hereby dismissed. The appeal filed by Dr. (Mrs.) Madhu Jain (respondent No. 4 in Writ Petition No. 802 (S/B) of 2001) deserved to be allowed and is accordingly allowed. Her selection, recommendation and appointment as Assistant Professor is held legal, valid and in accordance with law and could not have been set aside by the High Court. The order of the High Court to that extent is set aside upholding the action of the University. On the facts and in the circumstances of the case, however, all the parties are directed to bear their own cost

ppp

NINETEEN

NAIR SERVICE SOCIETY VS. DIST. OFFICER, KERALA PUBLIC SERVICE COMMISSION AND ORS., 2003

Hon'ble Judges/Coram:

V.N. Khare, C.J.,A.R. Lakshmanan and S.B. Sinha, JJ.

Equivalent Citation: 2004(16)AIC552, AIR2004SC834, JT2003(9)SC408, 2003(3)KLT1126(SC), 2004LabIC133, 2004(1)LLN51(SC), 2003(9)SCALE608, (2003)12SCC10, (2004)SCC(LS)1037, [2003]Supp5SCR551, 2004(1)SCT1(SC), 2004(1)SLR335(SC), MANU/SC/0928/2003

Relevant sections: Rules 14-17 of State and Subordinate Service rules, 1959 (Kerala rules)

Number of pages in original Judgment: 14

Case Note:

State and Subordinate Service rules, 1959 (Kerala rules) - Rules 14-17--Appointment to service--Once the main rank list stood exhausted by advising from the list of the candidates included therein the supplementary reservation list of reservation candidates also ceased to be in force as otherwise Rule 15(c) of the rules will be violated--Article 16(4) of the Constitution of India.

Brief Facts:

For appointment in the service of KSEB to the post of Sub Engineers, the Public Service Commission prepared a rank list of 177 candidates. Along with the rank list separate supplementary lists were also prepared. The list came into force in 4th July 1994. 150 persons were advised on 20th August 1994. On 21st December 1994 there was another requisition for 100 more names. Only 80 persons could be advised as with that all the candidates in the merit list were advised. Thus the P.S.C. advised in all 239 names, drawing 177 names from the main rank list and 62 names from supplementary list, which became necessary to fill up the alternate reservation vacancies in the cycle of rotation of appointment. In the total names of 239 candidates Service Commission had resorted to the supplementary list for getting reservation candidates and Nos. 1 to 18 among the supplementary list of Muslims were advised. No. 19 onwards could not be advised as the main rank list got exhausted in the meanwhile. Out of the candidates advised 20 persons did not join duty which consisted of 11 open competition candidates, 3 S.Cs., three Ezhavas (O.B.C.) and 3 Muslims. The Non-joining Duty vacancies (N.J.D.) were reported to the P.S.C. for advise on 20th June 1995. As the main rank list had exhausted by that time no advice was made. Therefore No. 19 in the Muslim supplementary list who claimed appointment to one of these N.J.D. vacancies of Muslims, he being the next unadvised candidate in the Muslim Supplementary list filed O.P. 12305 of 1995 in the Kerala High Court for direction to the P.S.C. to advice candidates to the N.J.D. vacancies of Muslims. This was followed by similar other writ petitions. The stand taken by the P.S.C. was that once the main rank list stood exhausted by advising the last of the candidates included thereon, the supplementary list of reservation candidates also ceased to before in force as otherwise the Rule 50:50 will stand violated. A learned Single Judge allowed the Writ Petitions and directed the Respondent therein to appoint them in the NJ.D. vacancy. Aggrieved the Service Commission filed appeal as W.A. 582 & 583 of 1997. A Division Bench of the High Court dismissed the appeals and directed the Respondents to issue advise memo to appoint these without going into the question whether the limit of reservation would exceed 50 per cent and such matters. The Appellant--Society was not a party before the High Court. The Appellant--Society sought leave to file the appeals. The reason given was that the Public Service Commission which had lost in the High Court was not filing any appeal against the judgment which was against the interest of the public and that therefore N.S.S. is filing the appeal bona fide in public interest. The Supreme Court directed to issue notice to the Respondents and granted leave thereafter.

Held, while allowing the appeal;

Per Lakshmanan, J. (for himself and on behalf of the Chief Justice).-- The impugned judgment, in our opinion, did not appreciate the well-settled principles of the law that the court should not substitute the provision of a statute by its own decision. In this case, the impugned judgment ignored the provisions of statutory rules to substitute the decision in the place. The K.S. and S.S. rules, 1959 lays down the principle of reservation under Article 16(4). The rules laid down the principle and the procedure if followed in giving effect to the reservation for Scheduled Castes and Scheduled Tribes and Backward Classes in the State. Rule 15 refers to the integrated cycle of rotation and it deals with the procedure to be adopted in selections where any candidate may become available for recruitment from the reserved group. This Rule lays down the principle of limitation of percentage of reservation including the carry forward. The reservation of vacancies including carry forward vacancies shall not exceed 50 per cent of the total number of vacancies for which selection by direct recruitment to that category is resorted to in that year. Rule 16 provides that there is sub-rotation among O.B.Cs. Rule 17 enumerates the sub groups among O.B.Cs. mentioned in Rule 14(a) and Rule 16. Throughout these rules, there are clear indications that the scheme of reservation followed in the State of Kerala under direct recruitment is with respect to vacancies. Rule 14(c) lays down the manner of making appointments. Rule 15 also makes it clear that appointment referred to is with reference to vacancies as made out in the proviso under Rule 15(c) and the note thereunder. The judgment of the High Court proceed on the wrong premise that the principle of reservation is with reference to the post. In our view, Rules 14-17 do not contemplate making supplementary list and the statutory rules envisage making a ranked list which is defined in Rule 2(g) of the K.P.S.C. Rules of Procedure. The definition in Rule 2(9) shows that there is only one ranked list. Therefore, the supplementary list prepared by the K.P.S.C. to satisfy the rules of reservation has, in fact, no statutory backing. For that reason when the main list is exhausted or expired, supplementary list cannot be allowed to operate. If the supplementary list alone is allowed to operate it would amount to giving greater sanctity to it and long life than the main list prepared in accordance with the Rules. Secondly, after the expiry or exhaustion of the main list if the supplementary list is operated it would violate the first proviso to Rule 15(c) of the General Rules.

We are, therefore, of the opinion that the High Court is not correct in its conclusion that the Respondents would be entitled to appointment based on the supplementary list. Question No. 1 is answered in the negative. Likewise, it is not open to the High Court to exceed percentage of reservation beyond 50 per cent against the statutory protection.

Per S.B. Sinha, J. (Concurring).--The judgment of the High Court, if implemented, would thus be violative of Article 16(4B) of the Constitution as also me statutory rules.

The High Court, therefore, committed an illegality in passing the impugned judgment insofar as it failed to take into consideration that in the event the same is given effect to, more than 50 per cent of the vacancies in a particular year will be filled up from amongst the reserved category candidates.

ppp

TWENTY

STATE OF BIHAR AND ORS. VS. BAL MUKUND SAH AND ORS., 2000

Hon'ble Judges/Coram:

S.B. Majmudar, G.B. Pattanaik, V.N. Khare, U.C. Banerjee and R.P. Sethi, JJ.

Equivalent Citation: AIR2000SC1296, JT2000(3)SC221, 2000LabIC1389, 2000(2)PLJR83, 2000(2)SCALE415, (2000)4SCC640, (2000)SCC(LS)489, [2000]2SCR299, 2000(3)SCT459(SC), 2001(1)SLJ275(SC), 2001(2)SLJ1(SC), 2000(2)SLR448(SC), MANU/SC/0195/2000

Relevant sections: Articles 16, 233, 234 and 309 of Constitution of India and Section 4 of Bihar Reservation of Vacancies in Posts and Services (For Scheduled Castes, Scheduled Tribes And Other Backward Classes) Act, 1991

Number of pages in original Judgment: 77

Case Note:

Constitution - interpretation - Articles 16, 233, 234 and 309 of Constitution of India and Section 4 of Bihar Reservation of Vacancies in Posts and Services (For Scheduled Castes, Scheduled Tribes And Other Backward Classes) Act, 1991 - matter raises question of interpretation of provisions of Articles 233, 234 and 309 - State proposal to provide reservation on ground of inadequate representation of certain backward classes if considered adversely affect efficiency of administration - such exercise under Article 16 (4) not permissible - this is constitutional limitation on exercise of enabling power of reservation under Article 16 (4) - creation of cadres and creation of posts comprised in judicial service can be resorted by Governor in exercise of rule making power under Article 309 any vacancies in create posts to be filled only after following procedure laid down by Articles 233 and 234 and cannot be subjected to any other procedure - mandate of Section 4 gets directly hit by scheme of Code as envisaged by Articles 233 and 234 - such mandate impinge upon power of High Court in suggesting appointment of suitable candidates to fill up posts of judicial officers with view to fructify goal of furnishing effective mechanism of judicial administration and making judiciary fully vibrant, effective and result oriented - such independent judiciary is heart of constitutional scheme - impugned mandate not applicable to judicial services.

Brief Facts:

Facts leading to Civil Appeal No. 9072 of 1996:

This Court, by its order dated 13th October, 1993 in Civil Appeal Nos. 4561-62 of 1992 (reported in MANU/SC/0169/1994 : AIR1994SC765 in State of Bihar v. Madan Mohan Singh, had quashed the earlier advertisement for filling up the vacancies of Additional District Judges in the District Judicial Service of Bihar and directed the appellant State to fill up the same through a fresh advertisement. In the mean time, it appears that as the High Court had not agreed to the suggestion of the State authorities to have reservation in the posts of District Judges for reserved category of candidates and had insisted on proceeding with the recruitment as per the 1951 Rules, styled as the Bihar Superior Judicial Service Rules, 1951, which were framed by the Governor of Bihar in exercise of the powers conferred by the proviso to Article 309 read with Article 233 of the Constitution of India and which Rules did not provide for any such reservation, the Governor of Bihar issued the impugned Ordinance which subsequently became the impugned Act by which the scheme of 50% reservations for reserved category of candidates was directed to be applied while effecting direct recruitment to the posts concerned. On 16th November, 1993, the appellant State requested the High Court to effect recruitment to the vacancies in the cadre of District Judges on the basis of the reservation provided by the Ordinance which subsequently was followed by the Act. By its communication dated 16th December, 1993, the High Court of Patna insisted that recruitment to District Judiciary can be made on the basis of 1951 Rules only. By a communication dated 5th April, 1994, the High Court informed the authorities concerned that no reservation of posts in the district cadre could be implemented and while making appointments from the members of the Bar for direct recruitment, preference may be given to the Scheduled Caste (for short 'SC') and

Scheduled Tribe (for short 'ST') candidates who are of equal merit with general category candidates. On 7th April, 1994, the High Court intimated that there are 54 vacancies in the district cadre which had to be filled up. The State Government, however, issued the impugned advertisement of 16th June, 1994 by which 50% of the available vacancies of District Judges were sought to be filled in from reserved category of candidates and the remaining 50% posts thereof, i.e. 27, were to be filled in by the open category candidates. It is this advertisement which was challenged by the writ petitioners before the High Court. The High Court, by the impugned judgment as noted earlier, has allowed the writ petition and quashed the condition of reservation sought to be imposed by the impugned advertisement.

Facts leading to Civil Appeal arising out of S.L.P. (C) No. 16476 of 1993:

By a proposal dated 30th January, 1991, the appellant-State consulted the Bihar Public Service Commission regarding making provision for reservation of posts in the Subordinate Judicial Service for reserved category of candidates. The said proposal of the appellant-State was also placed for consideration of the High Court but it was not accepted by the High Court by its communication dated 16th April, 1991, and that resulted in the impugned Ordinance, being 33 and 34 of 1991, which were followed by the impugned Act. The original writ petitioners, who had already appeared at the competitive examination in April, 1991 moved the High Court challenging the Ordinances and the latter Act in so far as the scheme of 50% reservation of posts for direct recruitment at grass root level of the State Judiciary was concerned. As noted earlier, the aforesaid writ petition was allowed and relief was granted against the appellants.

Held, while allowing the petition:

The High Court is thus held to have fell in error of law in declaring the Act as ultra vires in so far as its applicability to the judicial service is concerned, and also in the matter of interpretation of its various provisions. The appeals are accordingly allowed by setting aside the judgments impugned therein with a direction to the respondents to fill up the vacancies in accordance with the Rules applicable and the provisions of the impugned Act without disturbing the appointments made till date on the basis of this Court's order. The seniority of the members of the Judicial service shall be determined in accordance with the Service Rules applicable and the provisions of the Act by adjusting the candidates selected on reservation to fill in the reserved slots keeping in view the quota and rota rule as specifically pointed out by this Court in its order dated 16-11-1996. No costs.

Leave granted. The Civil Appeals stand dismissed as per the majority view subject to the modifications and directions contained in the main judgment. There will be no order as to costs.

ppp

Videos & Tv Shows On Law & Exim

List of some important videos & TV shows on Law & EXIM by Adv. Jayprakash Somani on his YouTube Channel 'Jayprakash Somani EXIM & Legal'

Legal Videos: Hindi -English

1) SLP in Supreme Court / Special Leave Petitions in the Supreme Court of India

2) Transfer of Civil & Criminal Cases by the Supreme Court of India / Transfer of Matrimonial Cases

3) Appellate Jurisdiction of the Supreme Court of India

4) Jurisdictions of the Supreme Court of India

5) Public Interest Litigation in the Supreme Court of India / PIL in Supreme Court

6) Article 32 Writ Petitions in the Supreme Court of India

7) Bail Matters Top 10 Supreme Court Cases

8) FIR Quashing in High Court & Supreme Court

9) Bail & Anticipatory Bail Matters in Supreme Court

10) Insolvency & Bankruptcy Matters in the Supreme Court

11) Insolvency & Bankruptcy Code 2016 Part 1

12) Insolvency & Bankruptcy Code 2016 Part 2

13) Insolvency & Bankruptcy Code 2016 Part 3

14) Corporate Liquidation Process

15) Supreme Court Rules & Procedures Webinar of 2.5 hour on Zoom

16) RDDBFI Act, 1993 (Introduction)

17) The Indian Contact Act 1872

18) Negotiable Instruments Act (Introduction)

19) How to avoid matrimonial disputes& some more videos

20) SEBI Matters in the Supreme Court

21) Matrimonial Matters: Supreme Court's 20 Case Laws

22) Consumer Matters Supreme Court's 20 Case Laws

23) Service Matters Supreme Court's 20 Case Laws

24) How to Search Lawyer for Your Matter

25) Property Matters Supreme Court's 20 Case Laws

26) Bail Matters: Supreme Court's 20 Case Laws

27) Supreme Court / High Court Vacation Benches

28) 69000 Teacher's Recruitment Matters of UP Government in the Supreme Court

29) Contempt of Court Matters in the Supreme Court

30) Advocate Act's Matters in the Supreme Court

31) Business Law Matters in the Supreme Court

32) Banking Matters in the Supreme Court

33) Labour Law Matters in the Supreme Court

34) Arbitration Matters in the Supreme Court

35) Careers in Law -Zoom Webinar by Adv. Jayprakash Somani

36) Civil Matters in the Supreme Court

37) Consumer Protection Act | Consumer Matters in the Supreme Court

38) Corporate Matters in the Supreme Court

39) Criminal Matters in the Supreme Court

40) Role of Respondent in the Supreme Court of India

41) Motor Vehicle Accident Matters in Supreme Court with case laws

42) Article 131 Original Suits in Supreme Court

43) PIL in Supreme Court/ Public Interest Litigations in the Supreme Court of India'

44) CAB Citizenship Amendment Bill is not Unconstitutional

45) Supreme Court of India Cases & Process – Marathi

46) Legal Services Export / Export of Legal Services

47) Transfer of Matrimonial Cases by the Supreme Court of India

48) Public Interest Litigation PIL

49) The Specific Relief Act (Introduction)

50) Corporate Insolvency Resolution Process CIRP

51) ABMM's Career 5 - Careers in Law

52) Transfer of cases by Supreme Court

53) Writ Petitions in High Court & Supreme Court of India

54) Supreme Court Jurisdictions - Appeals, SLP, Writ Petitions, Transfer, Original, Review, Curative

55) LEGAL INDIA TV Show: Cases Handled in Supreme Court

56) Corporate Liquidation Process

57) Legal Services Export / Export of Legal Services

58) Corporate Laws

59) Election Matters- Supreme Court's 20 Case Laws

60) Companies Act, 2013

62) Competition Act, 2002

63) Banking Matters - Supreme Court's 20 Case Laws

64) Election Matters in the Supreme Court

65) Armed Forces Tribunal Matters in the Supreme Court

66) Compassionate Appointment Service matter

67) Foreign Exchange Management Act FEMA

68) Foreign Trade Policy 2021-26 Proposed

69) Customs Act 1962

70) Narcotic Drugs and Psychotropic Substances Act, 1985 NDPS Act

71) Foreign Trade Development & Regulation Act, 1992

72) How to Search Good Advocate in the Supreme Court of India

73) Sr. Adv Vikas Singh's Interview in Nani Palkhivala Wednesday Law Club

ᐅᐅᐅ

EXIM Videos: Hindi -English

1) Yes, I can do Import Export Business Easily! 36 points excellent video in Hindi

2) Yes, I can do Import Export Business Easily! 36 points excellent video in English

3) Import Export Business – Hindi video

4) Import Export Business - English video

5) Export Import Marathi TV Interview

6) Scope for Commerce Students in International Business- TV Show

7) Scope for Management Student in International Business- TV Show

8) Scope for Engineering Students in International Business – TV Show

9) Women in International Business- TV Show

10) How to do Import Export Business Successfully!'

11) Where one can get full information on Import Export Business?

12) What to do import & export?

13) Import Export Workshop/ Training/Course/ Diploma

14) How to Start Import Export Business & How to grow it. Live Webinar

15) Success Stories & Failure Stories in Import & Export Business

16) For MSME Scope in Export & Import...

17) Exports In Agri. & Food Products – English & some more videos

18) Exports to Dubai, Aabudhabii. e. UAE

19) Jewellery Exports from India

20) How to attend EXIM workshop to become excellent Exporter

21) Import Export Best Training Course – Online & Offline

22) Agri Product Export

23) Scope for Woman in International Business

24) Management Graduates Scope in International Business

25) Pharma Product's Export

26) Best Import Export Course | Practical Training | Aaronica Global Exim

27) Import Export Business for Commerce Graduates

28) How Do I Get Export Orders? Finding International Buyers

29) What Is APEDA In Import Export Business?

30) Which Is The Best Product To Export From India?

31) EXIM Remark by Manoj Kumar Faridabad

32) EXIM Remarks by Mahesh Telangana

33) What Licenses I Need To Start Import/ Export?

34) How Can I Increase My Import Export Business?

35) Which Is Best B2B Website For Import/Export Business?

36) Export Import Management with Global Marketing

37) How to Start Export Import Business | 51 Points Video

38) Scope for Commerce & Other Graduates in International Business

39) BE A SUCCESSFUL EXPORTER FOR OUR NATION - Marathi video

40) Export of Textile , Cotton, Agri., Food, & other products & services

41) Exports from MP, CG, MH, GJ & CA in Fresh Fruits & Vegetables

42) Exports in Agri. & Food Products- Hindi

43) Start your Online/E-Commerce Business

44) How to Start Export Import Business & Grow it

45) Exports in Textile & Other Products

46) Start and grow EXIM business - Live English Webinar

47) 'Import Export Business!' Why, Who, What & How can one do it easily!!

48) Live: Export of Product & Services During & After Lock Down Period

49) Frauds in Import Export Business

50) Import Export for Business Man

51) Import & Export for Women

51) Import & Export for Graduate & Post - Graduate Students

52) Agriculture Exports from India

53) Digital Marketing Setup - Marathi

54) 2nd Secret of Successful Businessman

55) Digital Marketing Set up

56) Legal Services Export / Export of Legal Services

57) Export & Import with UAE

58) Service Exports / Exports by Service Providers

59) Import Export Workshop/ Training/Course/ Diploma

60) Exports & Imports with USA

61) Selection on Product for Export

62) Top Products Exported from India

63) What to do import & export?

64) ABMM Career 2 - 'Careers in Business & Industries

65) How to do Import Export Business Successfully!'

66) 5 Secrets of Successful Businessman

67) Export from MP, Chhattisgarh & Vidarbha Nagpur

68) EXIM Hindi - Textile & Apparel Export

69) EXIM Hindi - Export Import Practical Training In Delhi, Kolkata, Mumbai and Pune

70) Import Export Business

71) Import Export Business Hindi

72) Import Export Business English video

73) Import Export Business Marathi

74) Women in International Business by Exim Guru Adv. Jayprakash Somani

75) Opportunities in Foreign Trade- Adv. Jayprakash Somani's special interview

76) Textile Exports

77) India's Number in Exports. How to improve it?

78) 11 Benefits of Exim Workshop

79) Export Import Management with Global Marketing- 13 days Training Workshop

80) Cosmetic's Export

82) Export After COVID

83) Spices Exports

84) Handicraft Export

85) 10 Products India Exports to the World

ϷϷϷ

List Of Adv. Jayprakash Somani's Books

1. Supreme Court of India's Leading Case Laws on 'Insolvency & Bankruptcy Code 2016'
2. Bail Matters – Supreme Court's Latest Leading Case Laws
3. Arbitration Matters- Supreme Court's Latest Leading Case Laws
4. Property Matters - Supreme Court's Latest Leading Case Laws
5. Matrimonial Matters- Supreme Court's Latest Leading Case Laws
6. Election Matters- Supreme Court's Latest Leading Case Laws
7. SEBI Matters- Supreme Court's Latest Leading Case Laws
8. Banking Matters- Supreme Court's Latest Leading Case Laws
9. Service Matters- Supreme Court's Latest Leading Case Laws
10. Contempt of Court Matters- Supreme Court's Latest Leading Case Laws
11. Consumer Protection Matters- Supreme Court's Latest Leading Case Laws
12. Corporate Law- Supreme Court's Latest Leading Case Laws
13. Supreme Court's AOR Exam- Leading Cases
14. Armed Force Tribunal - Supreme Court's Latest Leading Case Laws
15. Acquittal From 376 - Supreme Court's Latest Leading Case Laws
16. Negotiable instrument – Supreme Court's Latest Leading Case Laws
17. Contract Act- Supreme Court's Latest Leading Case Laws
18. Insider trading- Supreme Court's Latest Leading Case Laws
19. Foreign Exchange and Management Act- Supreme Court's Latest Leading Case Laws
20. Income Tax Act- Supreme Court's Latest Leading Case Laws
21. Company Law- Supreme Court's Latest Leading Case Laws
22. Competition & Monopoly Matters- Supreme Court's Latest Leading Case Laws
23. Compassionate Appointment- Service Matters- Supreme Court's Latest Leading Case Laws
24. Compulsory Retirement- Service Matters- Supreme Court's Latest Leading Case Laws
25. Voluntary Retirement- Service Matters- Supreme Court's Latest Leading Case Laws
26. Removal/Dismissal/Termination from Service- Supreme Court's Latest Leading Case Laws

27. Seniority- Service Matter- Supreme Court's Latest Leading Case Laws

28. Promotion- Service Matter- Supreme Court's Latest Leading Case Laws

29. Equal Pay for Equal Work- Service Matter- Supreme Court's Latest Leading Case Laws

30. Condition of Service- Service Matter- Supreme Court's Latest Leading Case Laws

31. Customs Act- Supreme Court's Leading Case Laws

32. Information Technology Act- Supreme Court's Leading Case Laws

33. SEC. 125 CR. P. C.- Supreme Court's Leading Case Laws

34. SEC. 498A OF I. P. C.- Supreme Court's Leading Case Laws

35. MOTOR VEHICLE ACT- Supreme Court's Leading Case Laws

36. CONDITION OF SERVICE- SERVICE MATTER- Supreme Court's Leading Case Laws

37. SUSPENSION- SERVICE MATTER- Supreme Court's Leading Case Laws

38. Reservation in SC, ST, OBC- Service Matter- Supreme Court's Leading Case Laws

Books are available online in India

1. Notion Press: https://notionpress.com/author/jayprakash_somani

2. Amazon: https://www.amazon.in/s?k=jayprakash+somani

3. Flipkart: https://www.flipkart.com/search?q=Jayprakash%20Somani

Books are available online at International Market

4. Amazon International: https://www.amazon.com/s?k=jayprakash+somani

5. Amazon United Kingdom: https://www.amazon.co.uk/s?k=jayprakash+somani

6. E-Books/Kindle edition at National & International Level: https://www.amazon.in/s?k=jaypraksh+somani

ᑭᑭᑭ